The Super Handyman Homecare Almanac

Also by Al Carrell:

Best Home Hints from the Super Handyman

The Super Handyman Homecare Almanac

Al Carrell

Taylor Publishing Company
Dallas, Texas

To the thousands upon thousands of my readers,
listeners, and viewers who have heeded my advice
and become do-it-yourselfers . . . and to my wife, Jean,
who convinced me to try it.

Copyright © 1992 by Al Carrell

Published by   Taylor Publishing Company
                1550 West Mockingbird Lane
                Dallas, Texas 75235

Designed by Gary Hespenheide

Library of Congress Cataloging-in-Publication Data
Carrell, Al
   The super handyman homecare almanac / Al Carrell.
      p.   cm.
   Includes index.
   ISBN 0-87833-792-X: $14.95
      1. Dwellings—Maintenance and repair—Amateurs' manuals.
2. Do-it-yourself work.   I. Title.
TH4817.3.C368 1992
643.7—dc20
                                             91-46778
                                                 CIP

10 9 8 7 6 5 4 3 2 1

The Super Handyman Homecare Almanac

IMPORTANT PHONE NUMBERS

Electrician _____ Plumber_____
Air Conditioning _____ Heating _____
Carpenter _____ Chimney Sweep _____
Roofer/Repairs _____ Lawn Care _____
Swimming Pool Service _____ Paper Hanger _____
House Sitter _____ Baby Sitter _____
Recycling Center _____ Stump Grinder _____
Tree Surgeon _____ Carpet Cleaner _____
House Cleaning _____ Jack of All Trades _____
Veterinarian _____ Painter _____
Insurance _____

Appliances—Service Departments, Etc.

_____ _____
_____ _____
_____ _____

City Departments
Animal Control _____ Water _____
Sewage _____ Garbage _____

Utility Departments
Gas _____ Electricity _____
Telephone _____

Ambulance _____ Appliance Parts _____
Better Business Bureau _____ Drapery Cleaner _____
Dry Cleaner _____ Fire Dept. _____
Fumigation _____ Glazer _____
Hardware Store _____ House Wrecking Service _____
Landscape Service _____ Lawyer _____
Moving & Storage _____ Notary Public _____
Pawnbroker _____ Pest Control _____
Piano Tuner _____ Police _____
Septic Tank Service _____ TV Cable Company _____
TV Repair _____ Upholsterer _____
Automobile Club _____ Wrecker Service _____
Service Station/Mechanic _____ FBI _____

USEFUL 800 NUMBERS

Helpful 800 Numbers To Call For Assistance

Many companies have set up 800 numbers that you can call toll-free for answers to questions regarding their products. The numbers listed are only a few of those available. Most of these numbers are available during normal business hours, and the people managing the phones are usually very knowledgeable. If you wish to call a company not included, dial 1-800-555-1212, this number gives you the information operator for 800 numbers.

National Solar Hotline-U.S. and Puerto Rico	
Solar questions answered	1-800-523-2929
Pennsylvania	1-800-462-4983
Alaska and Hawaii	1-800-523-4700
OSHA	1-800-356-4674
Radon Consulting and Testing (EPA-approved)	1-800-553-2141
U.S. Consumer Products Safety Commission	1-800-638-2772
	1-800-638-8270
Hearing Impaired	1-800-492-8104

AT&T—Phone installation help	1-800-222-3111
Armstrong Floors—Installation and maintenance help	1-800-233-2833
Brinks Home Security Service	1-800-225-5247
DuPont Stainmaster—Cleaning and spot removal tips	1-800-DUPONT
Formby Furniture Refinishing—Furniture stripping and finishing help	1-800-FORMBYS
General Electric/Hotpoint Appliances—Appliance troubleshooting and repair	1-800-433-5566
General Electric Plastics—Working with Lexan	1-800-845-0600
Honeywell—Thermostat questions answered	1-800-328-5111
Hoover Vacuums	1-800-232-5848
J & L Appliance Parts Company—Parts for all name-brand appliances	1-800-338-1200
Mannington Floors—Floor care	1-800-FLOOR US
Meletio Electrical Supply	1-800-777-4993
Phifer Wire and Nail	1-800-633-5955
Sears Roebuck and Company	1-800-366-3000
Stanley Home Products Inc.	1-800-628-9032
Thompson's Water Seal—Deck and other exterior surface care tips	1-800-367-6297
Westinghouse Security Systems	1-800-762-7825
Whirlpool Appliances—Appliance troubleshooting and repair	1-800-253-1301

REMEMBER . . . All these numbers are subject to change.

INTRODUCTION

Whether you live in an apartment or a house, you'll probably find that caring for your home becomes a year-round, 365-day-a-year commitment.

Our *Almanac* just happens to cover that exact period of time. And it has home-type things for you to do each and every day. Of course, we can't exactly pinpoint when or even if you might need to do these different projects at your house . . . and besides, this *Almanac* isn't for any particular year but for every year . . . forever!

So we've tried to discuss projects in the general seasonal time of the year that sort of fits. As you'll see, many of the topics covered are not tied to a season and could be done at anytime of the year. The index will let you look up information on the particular crisis or catastrophe that has just come into your life.

As the Super Handyman, I've always felt it is my job to sell you on joining the Do-It-Yourself movement. And in this almanac I'll continue to nudge you in that direction. However, I know that not everybody is going to tackle each and every project around the house. Well, the *Almanac* will also be helpful even if you're going to get a pro to do the job.

The *Almanac* will tell you when maintenance chores need to be done. This preventive maintenance is extremely important because taking care of the little maintenance steps will often prevent big repair or replacement projects later on.

If, on the other hand, you need to hire a pro for one of those really big projects, wouldn't it make good sense to know a little bit about what will be involved? The *Almanac* can help on that point. If you know what the project entails and see just what the professional does, maybe you'll decide to tackle it yourself the next time around. Often, just getting the bill after the work is done is enough to make you at least think about trying to do it yourself!

Each day-to-day offering will also include at least one handy home hint. I'd like to take credit for these clever tricks, but many hints are from readers to my syndicated newspaper column, listeners to my various radio programs, or viewers to my TV efforts. Not everything in the *Almanac* is "nuts-n-bolts": there are bits of trivia, folklore, wisdom, and wit. I've also tried to tell you a thing or two that happened on each particular day.

I hope you enjoy this book as much as I enjoyed putting it together!

JANUARY

- *Clean or replace filters in forced air heating system.*
- *Inspect heating system for safety.*
- *Clean the filter in the hood over the range.*
- *Check the attic for condensation during colder days.*
- *Clean the exhaust duct from the clothes dryer.*
- *Cut firewood, as dormant trees have less sap.*
- *Write for gardening catalogs and plan for spring gardening.*
- *Transplant . . . but check with your nurseryman as some varieties need to be moved at other times.*

1

Your main chore for today is to watch 87 bowl games on TV. However, if last night's party resulted in a dropped cigarette that burned the carpet, and if the burn didn't go down to the backing, you can often use fingernail scissors to snip out the burned fibers.

COOL, MAN, COOL! Each year at 1 A.M. on New Year's Day, members of the Sheboygan Polar Bear Club take a dip in icy Lake Michigan. In honor of this bravery, here are some ways to take care of frozen water lines.

HELP FOR FROZEN PIPES

The best way to handle frozen pipes is to prevent the freeze from happening. Pipe-wrap insulation can certainly help. If you haven't done that and expect a sudden freeze, you can leave the faucets turned on a steady drip. Moving water is less likely to freeze. Also open cabinet doors under sinks to allow the warmer air in the room to get in under there. You could even place a small heater or a large-wattage illuminated bulb in position to warm the pipes where possible.

If the pipes are frozen, you may be able to restore the flow by thawing. Be sure to start by opening the tap at the frozen faucet. This allows pressure to escape as you thaw. Then work back down the line from the faucet. Where you can do it safely, you could use a propane torch, but a heat gun is much safer. Also, the heat gun can direct hot air into the walls where the pipe might otherwise be inaccessible.

Z-DAY If your last name begins with the letter Z, you're used to being the last name called on most alphabetical lists. On the first day of each new year, all of you "Z" folks are honored with your own day.

THIS DATE IN HISTORY
January 1, 1913, marked the inauguration of nationwide parcel post service by the United States Post Office. It's said that all but three of the packages sent that day have been delivered. . . .

2

Pack away all the Christmas stuff. HINT: Egg cartons make good protective containers for tree ornaments.

ONE MORE CANDLE on the cake of convict/evangelist Jim Bakker. For convicts everywhere, here are some tips on use of the hacksaw.

THE HACKSAW

The proper hacksaw blade can cut through most metals around the house. The blade should be installed with the teeth pointing away from the handle. The blade should be tightened in the frame so that it is rigid. Grip the handle and then use the other hand on the front of the frame and apply downward pressure on the cutting stroke. The hacksaw doesn't cut on the backstroke. Start your cut with a few light forward strokes, using the teeth at the first inch or so from the front of the blade.

Hacksaw blades sometimes break. Keep a few spares on hand by taping them to the top of the saw frame.

If you need to cut a wider slot, put one or more blades together in the frame.

If you're going to be sawing in tight quarters where there isn't room for the frame, keep in mind that the blade can be installed upside down.

Or, use the blade without the frame. Wrap electrician's tape around the end of the blade to give yourself a handle to hold.

Your strokes with a hacksaw shouldn't be fast and furious. More than about 40 strokes per minute can cause heat from friction that can ruin the blade.

THIS DATE IN HISTORY
In 1980, Bert Parks was fired as the host of the Miss America pageant.

3

A patent was awarded in 1888 on the waxed paper drinking straw. This item has some home handyperson uses that you'll like:

Did you ever wish the spout on a tube or cartridge of caulk was a little longer? Slip a large drinking straw over the spout and tape it in place. You'll have the extra reach and also will enjoy the flexibility of the straw.

Or, light the end of a straw to get extra reach for lighting pilot lights, gas logs, or hurricane lamp candles.

Split the soda straw to let hold a small nail or tack to keep your fingers away from the action. As soon as the nail is started, the straw will let go for you to hammer the fastener on home.

GET THE CAKE OUT OF THE FREEZER

Betty Furness, who used to do refrigerator commercials in the early days of TV, celebrates her birthday today. In her honor, here's a refrigerator tip!

A refrigerator runs much more efficiently and often quieter when it is level. Place your level side-to-side and also front-to-back. Most units have adjustable feet to allow for levelling. If not, use shims.

4

A FEW WORDS ABOUT NEW YEAR'S RESOLUTIONS

By now, you have probably already broken all your New Year's resolutions. It's alright. Everyone else is in the same boat.

That's why we have a special offer . . . *a second chance!* Not with the same resolutions but with some new ones that I will help you to keep.

First, for all you non-do-it-yourselfers who have never tackled any project, resolve to try one project. We're talking only one! However, make it a project that is easy—one that will not take too long. Maybe something like tightening the screws in a door hinge or painting a bar stool with a can of spray paint.

You see, if you'll resolve to do this, I know it'll work out right and you'll be going on to bigger and better projects.

Now, for all you experienced do-it-yourselfers, I want you to resolve to pick out a job that you think is too tough for you to do. Then I want you to find out what the steps would be if you were going to do that job. You're not going to resolve to do it . . . only to find out about it. Probably after you find out the steps, you'll decide that it's not as tough as you thought and you'll go ahead with it.

You'll find these resolutions are a lot easier to keep than the ones I used to always make . . . to quit smoking and to lose weight. I finally did quit smoking, but not because of a New Year's resolution. I'm still working on that excess flab around my waist.

5

THIS DATE IN HISTORY

The first steamboat went to sea (or would that be to river?) on the Red River in 1859. And speaking of steam, here are some hints if you're steamed up over your steam iron.

A PRESSING ENGAGEMENT

The steam iron is great but sometimes it runs out of steam. The most common cause is that mineral deposits in the water have clogged up the iron.

One of the best ways to remove these deposits is to drain the water from the reservoir and refill it with white vinegar. You will then let the iron convert the vinegar to steam and it will clean out the problem.

Since the iron has to be held down in a pressing position for the steam to be sent out, this could tire your arm if you had to hold the iron for that long. Take the broiler pan from the oven and place the iron on it. The cover has slots for the steam to pass through and the job will get done without your arm falling off.

After the steaming is done, use a pipe cleaner to ream out the holes on the bottom plate.

If the plate of the iron gets scratched up, you can often take very fine steel wool and smooth it. Then press over a sheet of wax paper and the iron will be good as new.

6

This is alleged to be the birthdate of the great detective, Sherlock Holmes. Even he didn't have a clue to our question of the day, which is . . .

WHAT'S A KILOWATT?

If you got a shock when you received your last electric bill, you might like to know a little bit about how the power company figures the bill. They charge you by the kilowatt hour.

Do you have any idea what the heck a kilowatt hour is?

Well, it's the equivalent of a thousand watts of power being used for one hour.

"What's a watt?" you ask.

A watt is a unit of force indicating the rate at which a device converts electrical current to something else . . . like heat, motion, light, or whatever. In other words, the rate at which a gadget uses energy. Many appliances have a wattage figure printed on an attached plate. Even light bulbs have a stamped-on wattage.

To find out the kilowatt hours, let's say, of a 100-watt bulb that is used 20 hours per month: 20 times 100 is 2,000 watts. To find out the number of kilowatts, divide that by 1,000 and you have 2 kilowatt hours. That's certainly not much, but when you add up all the electrical gadgets you have, you'll start to see why the bill is so big.

So, by finding the wattage on all your electrical gadgets and using the above formula, you might discover that some things you use a little too much may be responsible for running up the bill . . . maybe you'll see how to cut back on some of these big users and save some money.

7

THIS DATE IN HISTORY

The first patent on a typewriter was issued on this date in 1714.

In 1610, Galileo discovered the 4 moons of Jupiter, which ranks right up there with discovering a hidden hardwood floor in your old house.

OLD HOUSE TIP

A NEW FOUND HARDWOOD FLOOR

In restoring an older home, many folks will peel off carpet or linoleum and find a perfectly good hardwood floor underneath. Hardwood flooring is back and very popular so don't cover it back up . . . think about restoring it.

Most such old floors will need to be sanded and cleaned. A rented drum sander is probably the best way to go.

REFINISHING HARDWOOD FLOORS

The best way to remove an old worn-out floor finish is to sand it. Before you think about crawling around on your hands and knees to do this, you should know that tool rental places will have drum sanders that will let you stay erect for most of the process. That doesn't mean, however, that the job is now going to be a snap. The drum sander is a big machine and the good rental folks will make sure you know how to handle it properly before you leave.

Once you're home, here's the routine:

1. Haul everything out of the room, including furniture, drapes, and even wall hangings.
2. Tape over the heating and air conditioning vents and staple a plastic drop cloth over doors leading to other parts of the house. When you're ready to actually start sanding, open all the windows so that some of the sanding dust goes outside.
3. Carefully pry up the shoe molding so your sanding can get as close to the edge as possible.
4. Cover the entire floor looking for any nailheads that might be sticking up. Use a nailset to drive them below the surface.
5. The sanding process will usually require three cuts. The first uses a coarse sandpaper, the second uses medium, and the third uses a fine grit to leave the floor perfectly smooth. Sand with the grain for all three cuts.

The drum sander cuts very fast so you must never allow the sanding drum to contact the floor while the unit is stationary. Use the clutch lever to lift the drum before you stop.

For the final sanding, remove your shoes and work in socks or with crepe-soled shoes to avoid any shoe marks on the bare wood.
6. Since the drum can't get right against the wall, use an edger sander, which you can also rent. Be sure your dealer tells you how to best use this so you don't leave swirls.
7. Neither of these two power sanders can get into the very corners, so you'll need to do this by hand.
8. Sanding dust is a big problem. Vacuum the floor, the baseboards, window ledges, and any other surfaces where dust may have settled. You don't want any dust to float down on your wet finish. Also, the fine dust is highly combustible, so empty the dust bags outside and into boxes.

To decide if you'll need to stain the floor after sanding, wipe mineral spirits paint thinner over an area of about a square foot of the bare wood surface. This brings out the wood color and grain while adding depth. While this spot is wet, you will see just about what the floor will look like after adding a clear finish. If you want more color, add stain. If you decide the floor should be lighter, you'll have to bleach it. You can use either regular laundry bleach or wood bleach.

After staining or deciding it's OK as is, you must finish the floor. Varnish is popular but polyurethane has become the choice of many do-it-yourselfers. It's a little easier to work with and leaves a hard finish that is less likely to yellow than real varnish. Probably two coats will do. You might also add floor wax for extra protection.

The rich look of hardwood does have the disadvantage of being colder in the winter and noisier at all times. A nice oriental rug will take away those disadvantages . . . as well as a bunch of bucks.

8

TAKE TWO SIPS AND CALL ME IN THE MORNING

It is said that on this day in the year 354 B.C., Hippocrates, the father of modern medicine, first prescribed vinegar for a patient as a treatment of a flesh wound. He had already used vinegar as a cure for an upset stomach. His favorite medication, however, was honey. The first Hippocratic Oath was said to have included the phrase, "You can attract more flies with honey than with vinegar."

VINEGAR

Vinegar is no longer considered a medicine but it does cure a lot of problems around the house. For example, vinegar does a great job of removing water spots, mineral deposits, or soap scum from surfaces in the bath. Hot vinegar works even better.

- White vinegar and water, mixed equally, is a good spot remover on carpets, including pet accidents and the accompanying odors.

- After a party, put a dish of vinegar in the room to remove all the odors, including booze and cigarette smells.

- Vinegar is an excellent glass cleaner. Two tablespoons of vinegar per quart of warm water is a good solution.
- If you're an angler, get the fish smell off your hands with a vinegar rinse.
- Warm vinegar will soften up decals for easier removal. Soak a compress with vinegar and tape it over the decal.
- When there's not a rust remover around, soak the parts in vinegar and the corrosion will start to dissolve.
- Vinegar is also a good substitute for penetrating oil.
- Some old glues are dissolved by vinegar.
- A stiff paint brush can often be restored by soaking in vinegar. Follow this with a bath in detergent and water.
- Pour several gallons of vinegar into the water heater tank after draining to eliminate mineral deposit build-up. Be sure to shut off the heat source and water supply before draining.
- Pour a gallon of vinegar into the dishwasher and run it through a complete cycle without dishes to get rid of mineral deposits. Also does the same thing for the clothes washer.

9

THIS DATE IN HISTORY

In 1913, Richard M. Nixon was born. He may be best known for the Watergate break-in so here's a home security message.

WHAT BURGLARS LOOK FOR

Interviews with three burglars who are responsible for a combined total of over 5,000 break-ins reveal a list of things they look for in a prospective target . . . plus some things that may prompt them to go elsewhere.

Potential victims are often first spotted by their front yards. The crooks are after the deserted look. No car in the drive, newspapers in the yard, mail in the box.

To be sure there's no one at home, the burglar may go to a nearby phone and leave the phone ringing so it can be heard from outside when they get back. A phone answering device may foil this plan.

Leaving a radio on may make it sound like people are at home and send him along to a house he can be sure of. Timers can also turn lights on and off to make it seem that you're there.

A privacy fence is inviting. Once in the backyard, the thief is out of view, and can take his time figuring out how to break in. A locked gate may help. A barking dog will definitely help. Neighborhood watch groups are a good deterrent to crime.

Alarm systems are great because these guys don't like to call attention to the fact they are around.

Of course you want to have good locks on doors and windows. Deadbolts are a deterrent but a thief can still kick in a door if the frame is flimsy.

These three crooks are temporarily in the slammer but they'll be out and there are thousands more out there . . . so take care.

10

Today marks the birth of Ethan Allen, a hero of the American Revolution, who has a line of furniture named after him. In his honor, we dedicate these furniture care tips.

UPHOLSTERY CARE

Upholstered furniture, whether it's Ethan Allen or Gracie Allen, is usually expensive. So it's worth protecting.

Dirt that becomes imbedded in upholstery fabric can act as an abrasive and grind away at the fibers. So keep it clean with weekly vacuuming . . . and don't miss under the cushions and between the seams.

If there are loose cushions that are covered on both sides, turn them regularly.

Direct sun is bad for upholstery and can cause fading.

Get after spills as soon as possible. But, be sure to test whatever cleaner you'll be using on a skirt, back, or other obscure spot to be sure the cleaner won't do damage.

If there are wooden arms or legs, be very careful as you apply furniture polish so as not to get it on the fabric.

Spray-on fabric protection is a good idea and is easy to apply.

It's a good idea to have a stain chart which you'll find in any of a dozen books at the library. Put a copy of the chart as well as all the cleaning aids it calls for in a container and you'll be ready to come to the rescue when an accident happens. Like a sort of Johnny-on-the-spot.

The spill that you attack right away may never live to be a stain.

11   WASHING THE CAR IN WINTER? DON'T BE SILLY!

In the middle of winter, most of us don't worry about keeping the family car clean. After all, it's just going to get dirty again, so why bother?

Well, first of all, if you drive where the streets have been treated with salt or other chemicals to help keep 'em driveable, these chemicals can ruin your finish if left on very long. If you don't wish to run the family buggy through the car wash, at least turn the hose on and rinse the chemicals away. While you're at it, hose off the undersides because the chemicals are attacking the metal under there, too.

Cleaning your car also helps you to spot any scratches that may have been hidden under the coat of dirt. If left bare, the metal could start to rust. Most dealers can supply you with a tiny bottle of touch-up paint that exactly matches your factory finish. If you don't want to do this or even have it done right now, at least put a coat of wax over the scratches. If they're left until spring, you could have to buy your car a new and very expensive spring coat . . . coat of paint, that is!

12

In 1918, a blizzard in Nebraska caused temperatures to dip to a minus 37 degrees. It was the coldest day of the year for the area.

BRRRRR!

This could be the coldest day of the year where you are. It's usually only on such a cold day that the pilot light in your furnace won't stay lit. You hold down the red button while your thumb starts to fall off, but when you let go, the flame goes, too.

What can you do? That's usually a day when the repair guys are the busiest. Rather than wait in the cold, cold house, why not try to fix it yourself?

The most common reason for this pilot problem is a gadget called the *thermocouple*. It's a safety device that prevents gas from going

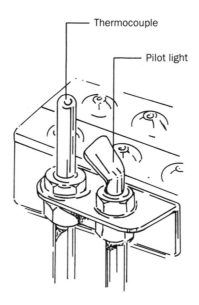

Thermocouple

Pilot light

to the furnace if there's not a pilot to ignite it. The thermocouple has a tube that sticks up right next to the pilot. The flame from the pilot should bathe the top quarter inch of this tube. If the flame isn't hitting it, that could be the problem. Reposition the tube tip.

It could be that the pilot flame is too low. Follow the gas line from the pilot back to the gas valve. There, you should find a pilot adjusting screw. See if you can get a better flame.

If that's not the problem, replacing a thermocouple is easy. The place where you buy plumbing supplies will have one and there are good instructions with it.

You can be warm as toast again before you can say, "Jack Frost!"

13

MORE BRRRRRRRRRR!

On a day when it's so cold outside that the cows are giving ice cream . . . and your furnace decides to give up. Bummer!

Until you can get it going again or crank up some auxiliary heat, it may help you to know how your body loses heat and thus maybe you can slow the heat loss.

Your body loses heat through radiation. The more your body is covered, the less area it has from which to radiate the heat away. The head is a big heat radiator . . . so a hat is important. You may feel silly wearing a hat in the house, but you'll be warmer.

The body also loses heat through convection. So wind-proof clothing will help. You might also want to stay out of the breezes.

Evaporation is another way your body makes you colder. As moisture evaporates from the skin, heat is lost. Layered clothing will breathe better and carry away perspiration without evaporation.

We also lose body heat as we breathe, letting that warm moist air out . . . but if you stop breathing, you'll have other problems. You can avoid heavy breathing by pacing your activities. It's also better to breathe through your nose . . . if it's not stopped up.

This is certainly not a medical report on how not to freeze your buns off . . . but maybe it'll help you to stay a little warmer until the heater kicks back in.

14

BURN, BABY, BURN!

Even though almost anything will burn in fireplaces and wood stoves, there are some things you should shy away from because they're not safe.

For example, the scraps of wood that you pick up at a building site might be treated wood. This type of wood has preservatives that can throw off all sorts of toxic fumes that may not all go up the chimney. And old painted wood could have lead in it.

Pine wood scraps are safe to use but this species does tend to build up creosote at a much greater rate than many other types. This can result in a flue fire.

Newspaper logs are used by lots of folks but unless you take out all of the pages printed with colored ink, you can be sending out cancer-causing smoke and fumes.

If you still have your Christmas tree in the backyard, resist the temptation to burn it in the fireplace. This wood burns too fast to give much heat and it flares badly. It too is a creosote creator.

So when you're looking for cheap fuel, make sure you don't end up with cheap thrills that send you up in flames.

15

THIS DATE IN HISTORY

In 1919, the Great Boston Molasses Flood occurred. A holding vat broke open dumping over 2 million gallons of the goo. This resulted in a morass of molasses over twenty feet high. Twenty-one people died a sweet death.

HOT SPOTS, COLD SPOTS

The most pleasingly heated homes are usually those with heat zones. This means that all rooms throughout the house are given the proper amount of warmth. In an existing house, it's not that inexpensive to redo a heating system so that this even heat balance is attained. There are some ways to help rooms that don't get enough heat. It's worth a try.

First, be sure that there aren't any obstructions to the flow of the hot air. Furniture that is too close to the heat registers might be the culprit.

Hot air ducts running through a cold attic should be wrapped with insulation and all the joints should be sealed with duct tape.

Sometimes rooms closest to the furnace are too hot and some others are too cold. You may help the situation by slightly closing the duct dampers or register louvers in the hot rooms.

Often, a room with no return air vent can be helped by cutting off the bottom half inch of the door to allow the air to be pulled out to recirculate through the furnace.

There are new duct inserts that close when a room gets to the desired temperature so the warm air is all directed to where it's still cool.

Balance the warmth and you'll be more comfortable.

16

THIS DATE IN HISTORY

In 1920, Prohibition begins. Without it, we'd never have heard of Elliot Ness.

FREE HEAT!

Since heat rises, you may have a lot of expensive heated air up against the ceiling. Unless you're in the NBA, it may not be doing you any good. If you have high ceilings, it's worth recycling that hot air. A ceiling fan with a reverse feature can be set at the lowest speed, sending the air along the ceiling. When it hits the walls, the air goes down where it can add to the warmth where it will do some good.

It's a hot idea to help save energy dollars!

17

Thomas Crapper Day! No. It's not a spoof. In fact, here's an explanation of this British holiday.

Yes, today is the big day . . . a national holiday in jolly old England and also a very big day around the Carrell household. I'd like to think it might eventually become a red letter day at your house. For you see, today is Thomas Crapper Day!

Thomas Crapper is the gentleman credited with the development of the modern flush toilet. He and his company were sanitary engineers by appointment to his majesty, the King. You might say he created the most practical throne a King ever had.

If you're joining in the celebration today, be sure to decorate the bathroom with the traditional red and blue streamers. Then, at the stroke of high noon, you should join in the time-honored 21-Flush Salute. The rest of the day is usually spent in partying.

For those who have not yet been caught up in the spirit of Thomas Crapper Day, at least get hold of a basic how-to plumbing book and read up on how the flush toilet works and on how you can take care of minor repair problems. It's the least you can do for this genuine hero . . .

Thomas Crapper, we salute you!

This is also the birthday of Benjamin Franklin, whose famous kite in a rainstorm bit helped electricity to reach its present state. Ben is also the Godfather of Almanacs with his *Poor Richard's Almanack,* which he published every year from 1733 to 1758.

18

In 1779, Peter Mark Roget, creator of the thesaurus, was born, debuted, had his genesis, etc.

HIDING YOUR GOODIES

While you read this, six burglaries will be committed. Most are of the grab-and-gallop variety: the thief grabs everything of value that he can find in about four minutes and then gets the heck out of there. He'll look in all the old familiar places like the cookie jar, under the mattress, or under the Jockey shorts in the back of the drawer.

There are better places to hide things! But here are some places in the home to *avoid.* The shop, kitchen, or garage all offer possibilities for a clever hiding ploy. However, don't hide in a tool box or power tool case. There are items the crook might take anyway, and wouldn't he be pleasantly surprised when he found your diamonds under the drill?

A broom closet might be good but a clothes closet is not because he might stumble on your hidden treasures while looking for furs. Anywhere in the dining room is also bad since you know a thief will go in there looking for the silver service.

The bedroom is the most ransacked room in the house. The den and living room are bad because that's usually where the crook finds your VCR and TV.

Hopefully, *you'll* remember where you hid all the stuff!

19 THE TRASH MASHER

The last time we remodeled our kitchen, we got every appliance known to man, including a trash compactor. This gadget has its place but I'm not sure it's in our home.

I've learned about the trash masher's shortcomings the hard way. For example, if you put very many glass bottles in, the broken glass can cut through the bag and you know when it will break . . . as you're carrying it toward the back door.

I also found that if we put very many heavy things in, it soon became too heavy for my wife, Jean, to carry. That meant I was back on garbage patrol.

Every once in a while, some foodstuffs get into the compactor and even though it has a deodorizer system, it develops a rank smell.

We could probably do without a compactor next time around, but if you're thinking about buying one, spend a week keeping track of your garbage. If you're into recycling cans and paper products, you're not going to put those in the unit. Food stuff doesn't belong either, so you may decide what you're throwing away doesn't warrant the extra expenditure. Maybe you can use the extra cabinet space to store something . . . like trash bags.

20 THIS DATE IN HISTORY

The first official basketball game was played back in 1892. Without that event, we might not today have "Air" Jordan, which is a sneaky way to lead into our topic for today.

SNEAKY AIR LEAKS

Baseboard molding is decorative but it is also there to hide places where the wallboard and the floor are not exactly a thing of beauty. These two surfaces usually don't meet so the baseboard covers the gap.

So, "OK," you say. "It's hidden and I don't have to worry about it." From a looks stand point, you're right. But those gaps may be acting as entryways for cold air and exits for your heated air. You may be fighting the cold while the gaps are relieving you of cold cash.

On a cold windy day, dampen the back of your hand and move it slowly along the exterior walls right next to the floor. Any air movement will have a cooling effect on your hand.

The best way to cure this ill is to remove the molding and caulk to seal the gaps. But before doing this, see if there's a way to caulk without removing baseboards. If there is shoe molding, it's sort of like a quarter round piece, maybe you can get by with only removing it. Any time you do have to remove molding, exercise patience so as not to break it or damage the wall.

Sealing these gaps could give you a nice warm feeling.

21

THE REPAIRMAN COMETH, MAYBE

In most cases, doing it yourself is going to save you money. In some cases, it may even save you considerable time. You see, right now, as you read this, there are a whole bunch of people who stayed home from work to be there when the repairman came. The tradesman promises to be there by 9:00, but then didn't show up until 11:08.

Now I understand how these things can happen. The repairman knows that his previous job should take less than an hour. What he didn't know was that his previous job not only would involve the work but also would involve explaining to the customer the reasons he has to replace the do-hickey instead of just repairing it. He also didn't know that in addition to replacing the do-hickey, the customer forgot to tell him about the vibration . . . which requires another half hour to repair.

Of course, often the tardiness is the repairman's fault.

The best way to avoid this total waste of time is to not be dependent on somebody else in the first place. So saving time is just one more reason you should at least start trying to do-it-yourself.

22

THIS DATE IN HISTORY

In 1901, Queen Victoria died. She was 82.

MAKING THE THRONE MORE REGAL

Toilet seats are being improved all the time. There are the heated models and the padded units. Some are even covered in fur. You can get 'em in all sorts of colors and designs, from school colors to landscapes. Toilet seats are now a fashion statement for the home.

If you find one that suits your fancy, you'll be happy to know they're easy to install. However, you're liable to find the old seat just doesn't want to come off. Corrosion may have cemented the nuts in place. Try penetrating oil first AND give it time to do its thing. Be careful that the wrench doesn't slip and break the bowl.

If the nuts won't budge, use a hacksaw to cut 'em off. Put masking tape on the side of the blade next to the bowl. Also, smear the surface under where the blade will be with petroleum jelly. These steps may prevent damage to the bowl. With the seat in the "up" position, saw through the head of the bolt.

With both bolts cut, you're ready to install the new seat. Applying a coat of petroleum jelly to the threads of the new bolts will prevent the corrosion so you won't have the same trouble next time. Don't over-tighten the new nuts as too much muscle could crack the bowl.

A new seat will make the best seat in the house even better!

23

KITCHEN FIRES FROM COOKING

One of the most common home fires is the kitchen grease fire. Let's say you're trying to copy the Colonel's secret recipe and you get the least bit careless. Suddenly, your skillet is in flames.

The first thing many people try to do is rush the skillet to the sink to turn on the water. This is one of the worst things to do because the water can cause the hot grease to splatter and the fire to spread. Probably the next worst thing is to try to take the fire outdoors. You cannot safely handle a flaming skillet.

Baking soda is great for dousing grease fires. It's a good idea to keep an open box close at hand. Another way to extinguish such a fire is to simply put a lid on the skillet and this will smother the fire.

If a fire starts in the oven, close the oven door and the lack of oxygen will usually cause the fire to go out.

Every kitchen should have a fire extinguisher designated for class B fires. Be sure it's in working order and that you know how to use it.

Remember, if a fire gets out of hand and you can't control it, the most important thing is to save yourself and your family. To heck with those chicken gizzards.

24

In 1935, the first beer was offered in a can. Since then, billions of empty cans have plagued our highways. If you're into recycling, you'll like our handy can crusher plan shown below.

THE RECYCLER'S CAN CRUSHER

In the recycling of aluminum cans, they take up less space if crushed flat. As a crushing device, you'll be hard-pressed to beat a strong leg and an old army boot. However, if you're tired of stomping, consider making our can crusher.

It's easy and all you need in the way of materials is:

> 2 scrap 2x4s, about 16 inches long
> 1 sturdy strap hinge and screws
> 2 low-profile jar lids (mine were from a jar of spaghetti sauce) plus screws to attach them
> 1 heavy duty screen door handle

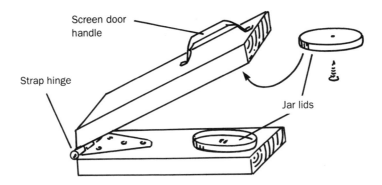

Screen door handle

Strap hinge

Jar lids

Look at the diagram to see how to put the crusher together. The jar lids will prevent the can from slipping out. The cans will crush easier if you bend the sides in slightly with a squeeze.

25 RADON ALERT

Is the radon gas scare for real? It's not just a scare, it's a fact of life for some homes. This invisible, odorless gas comes up from the ground and in the proper concentration could cause cancer. Testing is simple and not very expensive. And if you have radon gas in dangerous levels, it can be taken care of in most homes without too much trouble or expense.

Now, during colder weather, is a good time to test because your home is buttoned up tighter against the cold and also because of the vacuum effect from home heating. As hot air rises, it could help to draw radon gas up from the ground. Many heating systems—such as furnaces, fireplaces, and wood stoves—require intake air from inside the house. This will lower the air pressure inside which could cause an influx of air from below. In other words, now is the time when your home would most likely be showing the most radon gas if you have it.

You don't have to have an expert come into your home for the initial test. It's just a matter of placing the test kit. Be sure your radon test kit and the laboratory involved are EPA approved. Even if you don't have the problem, it's a relief to know for sure. Here's the phone number if you have questions—800/553-2141.

26 SMOKING IS HAZARDOUS TO YOUR HEALTH

By now, every one of you who is honest will admit to having started a fire in the fireplace without opening the damper. The reward for this foolish maneuver is a smoke stain on the front of the fireplace. Usually you can use detergent and water to remove smoke stains. But never use soap and water because soap leaves soap scum which won't look good at all.

If the stains don't respond, it's time for TSP. That stands for trisodium phosphate, a cleaner available in most paint departments. If TSP isn't available, ask for a TSP substitute. Mix about two tablespoons of TSP into a gallon of hot water. Wear your rubber gloves and get a scrub brush after the smoke stains. Rinse the area with plain water. Hopefully, all the evidence of your lapse of memory will be gone.

If you have some really stubborn spots, try making a paste of cream of tartar and water. Smear this over the stain and let it completely dry.

Maybe if you have to soak hard enough at getting out the smoke stains, it'll help you remember to open the damper next time.

27 OLD WOOD IS GOOD

Many people look at antique furniture as an investment. There are lots of old wooden furniture pieces that aren't in the antique class that may still be a very good investment because if you can buy it right, it can turn out to be a lot better than much of the brand new particle board and plastic laminate furniture that is on the market today. Much of this new stuff is over-priced and some not too well made. Often the old piece will be better made, even if it was mass-produced in a factory. If it's very old, they didn't have particle board or plastic, so it'll probably be real wood.

An old piece may have developed that look known in the trade as "patina" that gives the piece a look of warmth that you can't find in new furniture.

Often, a not too-well-cared-for piece only needs to be cleaned. Mineral spirits paint thinner will remove an awful lot of grime as well as waxy build-up. However, if it requires refinishing, you could still have the advantage of a well-made piece of furniture. If you do a good job of refinishing, you can have bragging rights about your skill for years to come.

28 WINTER SHOCKS

Winter weather can often play havoc with electrical power lines. A downed wire can be very dangerous. Maybe you've always heard that power lines are not dangerous because you can see birds sitting on them without any harm. Or, maybe you've heard that power lines are safe because they're heavily insulated. Or, how about the one that goes, you can't get a shock unless you touch two lines at once.

Any contact with a downed line should be considered dangerous: it is often fatal. The line can be carrying thousands of volts. If you spot a downed line, steer clear of it and warn others to stay away. Be sure it's reported to the power company.

The line doesn't have to be down to zap you. If you're installing a TV or CB antenna, make sure it doesn't contact any lines. Also make certain it couldn't hit the line if the wind blew it down. If you're into winter tree pruning, keep metal ladders away from the lines. The line bringing service into your home often hangs low enough that you have to be careful with pruners and loppers.

29 THE EXTENSION CORD OCTOPUS

For some reason, the electricians who wire new homes and apartments never seem to put the wall outlets where the eventual tenant wants to put the gadgets that are to be plugged in. So, we run an extension cord from the gadget to the outlet.

Before long, you could end up with an octopus of wires in every room. If you have to depend on extension cords, make every effort to take care of them.

While they are in use, see that they are not placed where people will walk on them or where furniture will be placed on top of them. Never run extension cords under a rug or carpet. Any of these situations can cause damage to the insulation around the wires which will create a hazard.

These cords should not be exposed to heat so don't place them where they can come in contact with things like a stove or heater and also keep in mind that motors in appliances can get hot enough to damage a cord.

Of course you don't ever want an extension cord to be exposed to water.

Many folks treat the cord with proper respect while it's in use but cause damage to it while it's being stored. When you store yours, be certain there are no kinks in the cord. Roll or wind the cord loosely so that there is no undue stress on the wiring. Don't hang it from a nail as the weight of the cord can crimp the wires over the nail. A large rounded holder is much better . . . like a nail through a wooden spool.

Store cords in a cool dry place that is protected from oil and grease.

When you need to use an extension cord that's been stored away, inspect it for cuts, kinks, and any other damage that could make it unsafe.

30 FALLING FOR YOU

Every year there are millions of parachute jumps and yet there are more disabling accidents from falls in the home than from skydiving. Immediately, you're probably thinking that I mean ladder falls and roof mishaps. Sure these things account for accidents, but there are other reasons that you might fall down. Here are some things to think about to make your home more fall-proof.

- Do you have any loose seams in the vinyl flooring? How about loose edges in carpets? Or, loose stair treads?

- Throw rugs can throw you and so they should be made slip-proof and should not be positioned where you might hit them on the run.

- All stairs should have hand rails and be properly lighted.

- A waxed floor looks great, but if it's too slick, it could be too bad for you! Also, if you spill water or grease on the floor, clean it immediately before somebody, maybe even you, slides into it.

- Slippery bathtubs should be made safe with the application of those slip-proof appliques that you stick on the bottom.

- Some falls are from tripping over carelessly scattered things like toys, magazines and papers, or furniture that's been moved out of place.

- Some real smooth concrete is slippery when wet. Try etching the surface with 10% muriatic acid solution to make it less dangerous.

If you're going to fall . . . it's better to fall in love!

31 WOOD IN WINTER

When we have our homes buttoned up for the winter, we often dry out the air inside. This lack of humidity can make you feel cooler than the temperature would indicate. This also can have a bad effect on wooden furniture. Drying the wood can cause loose joints, cracking, crazing, a lifeless look, and other problems. Today would be a good time to apply a protective coat of furniture polish or wax to all your furniture.

FEBRUARY

- *Clean or replace heating filter. (Yes, it's going to be an every month chore!)*

- *Vacuum coils on refrigerator.*

- *Run a gallon of vinegar through the clothes washer to remove all soap scum and mineral deposits.*

- *Check attic for condensation.*

- *Check snow on the roof for melting spots which would indicate heat loss.*

- *Paint radiators as heat makes for a longer lasting paint job.*

- *Run your sprinkler system as soon as it's warm enough. Check heads and look for leaks so you'll be ready when spring is here.*

1

THIS DATE IN HISTORY
In 1790, the first session of the United States Supreme Court convened. While the Supremes were waxing eloquent in their black robes, probably no attention was given to the floors. Let's address that subject now.

NO-WAX DOESN'T MEAN NO-CARE-FOR FLOORS

Most of the newer resilient floors that we used to refer to as linoleum are of the no-wax variety. Many people think this means you don't have to worry about taking care of the floor. While they are certainly low maintenance, the floor does need a little TLC.

Daily sweeping or vacuuming will rid the floor of dirt that could act as an abrasive to scar the tough finish.

Avoid using any abrasive cleaners but don't be afraid to damp mop with a mild detergent or even a diluted ammonia solution. Some manufacturers recommend their special cleaners for their type of flooring. Be sure to rinse well, as leftover detergent may dull the finish.

"No-wax" means no wax but when the sheen starts to go, you still have to apply a waxlike acrylic floor dressing. These products are even available at the supermarket. Maybe you're saying, "If you gotta do this what makes this finish better than the kind you waxed?" No waxy buildup to strip off is one big advantage. Another is that the acrylic dressing is harder than wax.

These floors are pretty much stain resistant but you should get after spills before they have even the slightest chance at becoming a stain. Most food spills and even acids can be wiped up with a damp rag or sponge. Use mineral spirits paint thinner, white appliance wax, or that waterless hand cleaner to remove rubber heel marks. Some solvents, like fingernail polish remover, lacquer thinner, and the like, could possibly damage the coating on these floors. These should be blotted up immediately.

All stains are not created equal . . . some are very stubborn. These include rust, blood, urine, grass, mildew, and asphalt. If the initial washing doesn't get the spot out, try using a product with oxalic acid in it, such as Zud or Barkeeper's Friend, available at supermarkets.

Rubbing alcohol will help on some stubborn spots and stains. You can also make a sort of compress from a folded paper towel soaked in a bleach solution of about ten parts water to one part bleach. Leave this in place for several hours, covering it with plastic to retard evaporation. It may draw out the stain.

"No wax" doesn't mean "no work."

2

In 1858, a patent was issued for waterproof boots. If you'd like to make your own waterproofing formula, read on.

WATERPROOFING FORMULA FOR BOOTS

Use a double boiler to heat 2½ ounces neat's-foot oil, 3/4 ounce mineral oil, and 1/2 ounce paraffin. This is a flammable mixture so take care. Stir this until all the wax is melted and the mix is well blended. Let the mix cool and then rub it into the boots with a rag. Be sure to get the mix well into the place where the sole and boot top meet.

> Today is Groundhog Day! No, you don't have to dig out a recipe for grilled groundhog. In olden days, it was believed that if the groundhog comes out on this day and sees his shadow, we're in for another six weeks of winter weather. Of course, we rational people know that this couldn't be factual. However, the groundhog has a better batting average than most TV weathercasters.
>
> Punxsutawney, Pennsylvania is considered to be the "official" seat of this traditional scientific event, and it has been an annual happening since 1887. Their groundhog, Punxsutawney Phil, is considered the king of weather prophets. (Eat your heart out, Willard Scott!)

3

THIS DATE IN HISTORY

In 1690, the first paper money was issued in what is now the U.S.A. Since money laundering is a popular sport these days, we chose the following topic.

THE WASHING MACHINE'S REVENGE

At times, I think that our home appliances may have human qualities. Like if a washing machine gets ticked off at the family, it'll start to chew up all of the clothes it's being fed. Or at least it seems that way.

When this happens, there's bound to be a more logical explanation, and with a little detective work, you'll find the reason.

The first thing to do is to check to see if the agitator is agitated. This device could be broken, cracked, or chipped and that could be the cause of damage to your clothes.

If there's no snag place on the agitator, slip an old nylon stocking over your hand and carefully rub over the entire surface of the tub. It should locate even the smallest burr or rough place. Once located, the snag place can either be smoothed with an abrasive or covered over with some sort of coating.

If you file or otherwise remove such a spot, be sure you haven't gone into the porcelain deep enough to expose bare metal. If you do, the formerly ripped up clothes will now start to come out looking rusty. To prevent this, cover the bare metal with epoxy paint or another waterproof coating. Not only would that spot rust, but water would start to work its way under the enamel on the tub and more of the coating could start to pop off.

Sometimes the problem is not in the washing machine. It's in the load. Zippers can chew up lots of things in a matter of minutes. So be sure to zip up your fly or whatever before you dump in any garments with a zipper. And if you have a handy person in the house, be certain to empty the pockets of nails, screws, and other small sharp items.

After all, those designer jeans cost too much to be gnawed into threads.

4

THIS DATE IN SEASONS

Today is generally considered to be the half-way mark in winter, so here's a tip that may prevent your falling on icy concrete. Instead of using chemicals to make the ice less slippery, take a load of ashes from the fireplace. Put them in the fertilizer spreader and distribute them over the concrete. Ashes will take the slide out. When the big thaw comes along, the ashes won't hurt your lawn as the chemicals often do.

5

In 1744, John Jeffries was born. Before you let out a resounding "So what!," this guy was considered to be the first weatherman. But without TV, what good did it do him?

BE YOUR OWN WEATHERCASTER

TV weatherpersons are often wrong. Maybe you'd like to be able to predict the weather yourself just as old-time farmers do. They let nature tell them what's going to happen.

For example, wasps build larger nests when there will be a colder winter. Unfortunately, many of us don't remember what size the nests were last year.

A white partridge perched on the highest limb means show is on the way. (Anybody ever see a white partridge?)

The wider the black band on a woolly-bear caterpillar, the longer and colder the winter will be.

Those old-timers could also read the snow flakes. Dry snow meant colder weather was on the way and wet snow meant a warming trend. If the falling flakes started to get larger, it meant that a thaw was on the way.

Our pets will develop a thicker coat if there'll be a colder winter.

6

SURF'S UP! In 1933, the highest wave ever recorded measured 112 feet. Even in smaller doses, water is the biggest enemy to most homes. It can rot wood; stain floors, walls, and ceilings; cause the foundation to fall; buckle floors; and do many other bad things. The water that does this damage can be from rain, plumbing leaks, underground streams, or even from the humidity in the air.

In the right places, water is great . . . so keep an eye out for water that gets where it shouldn't be.

7

Nobel-prize-winning author Sinclair Lewis was born on this day in 1885. One of his best known novels was *Main Street*. Whether you live on Main Street or wherever, your house number should be properly displayed. Otherwise, how will the bill collectors and process servers find you? Seriously, it's important in case of fire or other emergency for people to be able to quickly locate your address. If your number isn't well lit, luminous paint will help.

8

In 1990, Andy Rooney was suspended from the CBS *60 Minutes* show. Many times a TV program is not well received and sometimes the set goes out completely. TV repair isn't for the average person.

First, there is danger involved because the set stores power that could jolt you even if the set is unplugged. Secondly, if you don't know what you're doing, you could inflict even more damage.

Even if you don't know anything about TVs, there are some things to check. Be sure the set hasn't come unplugged. Then check the outlet to be sure it has current.

A bad picture could just be from the set not being properly tuned. Get out the owner's manual and fine tune. Another reason for a bad picture is the antenna. When weather permits your getting on the roof, be sure the unit is aimed properly. Look for loose or frayed wires coming off the antenna. If there's a bird nest built on the antenna, that could warp your picture.

Be careful on the roof so that when you get the antenna fixed you don't have to watch in a body cast.

9

In 1870, this day marked the establishment of the United States Weather Bureau. Their ribbon-cutting ceremony, planned for outdoors, is said to have been rained out.

WATER DAMAGE

Rain can be a pain. In fact, too much water from any source can flood your home. Get after the water as soon as it happens to minimize damage. Floors and carpets get the worst of it. Use a wet-dry shop vacuum to suck up as much as possible, but keep in mind that water and electricity don't mix. You'll probably have to remove carpeting so the padding and floor beneath can be dried.

If the entire room got flooded, you may do well to take the carpet and padding outside. Wet carpet weighs a ton so try rolling it up and sliding it out. Lay it out flat, bottom side up. When that's dry, flip it so the top dries.

Get fans going inside to dry the floor.

When everything is dry, you'll probably do well to have a pro relay the carpet to get it stretched right.

10

A rainy day is not all bad. It's a great time to go into the attic and really pin down the exact spot where the roof leak actually occurs. It's also a time to walk around the perimeter of your home to see if there are any places where water is puddling up. If so, you need to add soil so the grade will lead the water away from the house to avoid foundation problems. And another plus is the fact that you won't have to water the lawn.

THIS DATE IN HISTORY

Way back in 1863, the first fire extinguisher was patented. Do you have one? If not, here are some things you should know in buying one or more.

Fire extinguishers are marked with letters to indicate the type of fire they fight. The letters are A, B, or C.

The Class A fire is a common fire fueled by wood, paper, fabric, or rubber, and some plastics.

Class B fires are fueled by flammable liquids. A grease fire is also Class B.

Electrical fires are Class C.

There are also multipurpose extinguishers. One marked "ABC" would be good for the kitchen, where you could have grease fires, electrical fires, or common fires.

Keep the fire extinguishers in easy-to-reach places in all areas where a fire could happen. Make sure the units are checked regularly to ensure that they will work if needed. But remember, the most important thing is to get you and the other folks out alive and unharmed, so don't continue to fight a losing battle. The property can be replaced . . . people can't.

11

THIS DATE IN HISTORY

In 1889, the Department of Agriculture was created. While they mean well, the Department of Agriculture doesn't know everything. Here is some scientific data that may explain why you're not having luck growing things. Maybe you don't know about the influence the moon has on growing things. The signs of the zodiac also control whether you are a green-thumber or not.

According to moon experts, the best time to plant flowers and vegetables that bear their crops above ground is during the light of the moon. That is the time between the day the moon is new and the day it becomes a full moon. Bulbs and vegetables that grow underground should be planted in the dark of the moon.

The moon's place in the zodiac tells you when to best do many things in the yard. When the moon is in Aries, you should cultivate, plow, and till. The moon in Gemini indicates weeding. If it's in the sign of Cancer, watering is called for. In Aquarius, it's the best time to kill pests. Vines do best if planted when the moon is in Scorpio. Capricorn is great for planting potatoes. If you want a super onion crop, plant it while the moon is in Sagittarius.

If you don't understand all this, don't worry: neither did the Secretary of Agriculture . . . but he did read his horoscope.

12

John L. Lewis, the former leader of the United Mine Workers, was born on this day in 1880. If he'd had his way, we'd be burning coal instead of natural gas. If yours is a gas-fired water heater, help is on the way.

If the pilot light goes out, the same thermocouple problems apply here as with your furnace. See January 12 for some solutions.

Another common problem with a gas heater results from mineral deposits that build up on the bottom of the tank. This layer acts as insulation and makes it much more difficult for the burner to get the heat up through the layer to the water. Periodic draining will help eliminate this problem.

13

THIS DATE IN HISTORY

In 1769, Nicholas Cugnot invented a three-wheel, steam-driven vehicle. If he'd hung in there and perfected the method, we wouldn't be having to inhale all this polluted air.

TREES FIGHT BACK

While it's true that only God can make a tree, it's up to us to plant and nurture them. If you live in the city, there's even more reason to give God a hand because a tree can do some good things for our environment.

You probably already know that our insatiable use of fossil fuels creates millions of tons of carbon dioxide each year. This stuff is doing bad things to us as individuals as well as to our planet. Trees, on the other hand, thrive on carbon dioxide. Did you know that a single tree absorbs about 48 pounds of carbon dioxide per year?

Why not take a look at your landscape to see where a tree or two might look good. Usually trees will enhance the value of your property. In summertime, shade from the tree can help you to keep your cool and often save on air-conditioning bills.

After you've picked out the site, talk with a nurseryman about what trees are best where you live and when best to plant them.

14

HAPPY SAINT VALENTINE'S DAY!
Maybe you'd like to make a quickie breakfast-in-bed tray for your sweetie? If so, here's how to do it. Cut the top flaps from an appropri- ately sized corrugated box. Then cut out body-wide arches from the two long sides. Cover the entire piece with decorative peel-n- stick shelf paper and start cooking the Eggs Benedict!

15

THIS DATE IN HISTORY

In 1931, the first movie version of *Dracula* was released. This was before the present movie ratings were in effect. Would it have been rated R?

TODAY'S TOPIC IS R-RATED

Wait. Don't pass it by thinking we've gone porno, the R rating is for R-values, which stands for resistance values for insulation and other building materials. Insulation is rated in R-values. In each area of the country, there is an established R-value that is desirable for attics, walls, and floors. This is the amount of insulation you should have and that would be cost effective for the present utility rates for heating and cooling for your particular climate. If your home is underinsulated, the most effective place to add insulation in most cases is in the attic. However, you should know that the most productive dollar you can spend is the first one spent for the very first inch of insulation, whether it be in the attic, walls, or under the floors. For example, let's say that the old insulation provided you with an R-8. That cut out 87% of the heat loss through the attic. If you doubled that amount of insulation so you had an R-16, you would have stopped only 7% more heat loss or 94%. Now if you double that or create an R-32, you only have a 97% effective halt to heat loss. You can see that each additional quantity of insulation offers less and less return on the dollar. On the other hand, if utility bills continue to climb, the super insulation that you add now will certainly be a good investment in the future.

16

THIS DATE IN HISTORY

In 1943, Joltin' Joe DiMaggio joined the army. He would later be one of the world's greatest coffeemaker salesmen. If your coffee pot is turning out coffee that tastes like the inside of a baseball mitt, put in baking soda instead of coffee and run this through a complete brewing cycle. Then rinse completely and run plain water through the cycle. Your morning coffee jolt will be much better tomorrow.

17

OLD HOUSE TIP

In restoring an old house, you often want to get it back to the original look. If you don't know what the original look was, you face an impossible task. Why not canvass the neighborhood to see if any families have been there long enough to maybe have photographs with your home in the background?

18

Did you ever wonder when the first cow was transported by an airplane? Probably not. But it happened on this date in 1930, and when the stewardess offered, "Coffee, tea, or milk?," it was fresh milk because the cow was milked in flight.

COW POWER

To solve the energy crisis, maybe all electric power companies should check into what the utility company in Mill Valley, California, is doing. They have a power plant that can burn about a thousand tons of (are you ready for this?) cow manure per day. In doing so, they create as much electrical power as a thousand barrels of oil would do.

That's quite a savings. The area is home to more than 400,000 head of cattle, each of which creates almost 2 tons of "fuel" annually.

Now that's cow power!

Not all areas have this size cow population, but it's a great example of creative ways to cut down on our dependency on foreign oil. Why should we put some Arab potentate in the chips when we've got our own . . . cow chips!

19

THIS DATE IN HISTORY

Hey, music lovers, in 1878, Thomas A. Edison got a patent on the first phonograph. The following thoughts may be music to your ears by helping you fight the winter blahs.

PLANTS REMIND US OF SPRING

If you're getting cabin fever from being stuck inside during the winter, maybe some jazzy new houseplants will cheer up the family. This is also a great way to redecorate without buying new furniture or even repainting.

One thing you should know, however, is that when you bring in a new houseplant, it's a good idea to put it under quarantine for a few days. Why? Because it could have critters on it. Just keep the new arrival separate for two or three days while you look for and treat for bugs.

There is an old family recipe that you may want to use to make sure it's not going to start a bug epidemic throughout your plant kingdom. Here it is: Break off about 1/4 of a cheap but unsmoked cigar. Put this into a pint of boiling water along with a tea bag. Let this steep until it's cool. Then add 1/2 teaspoon of Listerine, 1/2 teaspoon of liquid detergent, plus 1/2 teaspoon of kelthane, which is available where you buy lawn and garden supplies.

Spray on leaves and stems, top and bottom. Then pour about 1/2 cup of it into the soil for any bugs hiding there.

Now when your new plant joins the rest of the family, they'll all get along great.

20

THIS DATE IN HISTORY

In 1962, John Glenn became the first American to orbit the earth. Before that, there'd been only monkeys, mice, and rats. Those rats were nice, but some are not.

YOU DIRTY RAT!

If you've been hearing the patter of little feet up above, it may be the family of rats or mice that has come to live with you during the winter. You can use poisons or traps to eliminate the pests, but if you don't find out how they got in, their cousins may soon take their place.

Look for openings around pipes or rotted spots behind rain gutters. Doors from basements or garages that have gaps under them may be the rodent entryway. Gaps in shingles let them get into your attic. Even missing mortar between bricks can let 'em in. Remember, they don't need much space.

You can use caulk, mortar mix, or wadded up steel wool to plug openings. After closing the entryways, check back after a day or so to see if they may have gnawed through your barricade.

You might also try to figure out what is so attractive to them. Chances are, you've been leaving food and water out for them. It may have been food scraps in the garbage, leftover food in pet dishes, or sacks of pet food in the pantry. It has been said that pests eat more pet food annually than our pets do. Take away the food and block their entry and you may start to live pest free.

21

To take a bite out of crime, the first burglar alarm was installed in 1858. I wish that every home had a security system, but whether you do or not, there are other things you can do to fight back.

One of the most important steps is to have dead bolt locks on all entry doors. These are usually easy to install and often go right into the same openings as the old inefficient spring-catch type. If not, you can add a dead bolt auxiliary lock just above the old lock. Two locks are better than one. *(See October 4.)*

Next, be sure all windows are locked. Then, drill a hole through the moveable sash and into the other one, but not through it. With a sturdy nail inserted in the hole, the sash can't be moved unless the nail is removed.

Make sure the exterior of your home is well lit and don't provide hedges or shrubs behind which a crook could hide while gaining entry to your home.

22

It was called a five cent store and it was opened by F. W. Woolworth in 1879. With inflation, it became the five and dime store, and now you'd be hard pressed to find anything that sells for a nickel, not even a package of gum.

The variety store has lots of little gadgets that can come in handy. Here are just a few ideas to get you ready for a trip to the five and dime.

Shower curtain rings have many uses. Put a few hooks over the hanger rod in a closet to hold belts, scarves, an umbrella, and other small items. Or, use a hook as a key ring that can hang from a pegboard wall in the shop to keep keys handy for outside gates, etc.

Cheap metal bread pans from the variety store can become under-shelf drawers. Attach metal tracks to the bottom of the shelf and the bread trays slide in and out easily.

A turkey baster can help add water to the cells of a car battery without any mess.

Plastic ice trays are inexpensive and are great benchtop holders for tacks, nails, screws, nuts and bolts, as well as other small shop items.

23 Composer George Frederick Handel was born on this day in 1685. Make a good "handel" for your file by poking the sharp point into a rubber bike pedal.

24

	WINDCHILL TABLE											
	—courtesy of Mount Washington Observatory, Gorham, New Hampshire											
Wind Velocity (MPH)	**Temperature (°F)**											
	50	41	32	23	14	5	–4	–13	–22	–31	–40	–49	–58
	Equivalent Temperature (°F) **(Equivalent in Cooling Power on Exposed Flesh under Calm Conditions)**											
5	48	39	28	19	10	1	–9	–18	–27	–36	–51	–56	–65
10	41	30	18	7	–4	–15	–26	–36	–49	–60	–71	–81	–92
20	32	19	7	–6	–18	–31	–44	–58	–71	–83	–96	–108	–121
30	28	14	1	–13	–27	–40	–54	–69	–81	–96	–108	–123	–137
40	27	12	–2	–17	–31	–45	–60	–74	–89	–103	–116	–130	–144
50	25	10	–4	–18	–33	–47	–62	–76	–90	–105	–119	–134	–148
	Little Danger				**Increasing Danger**			**Great Danger**				
	Danger from Freezing of Exposed Flesh (for Properly Clothed Person)											

25 The year was 1913. It was a black day for America because the Income Tax became effective.

WHAT'S YOUR HANG-UP?

When it comes to hanging things on the wall, too many of us believe that the old adage, "What goes up must come down," has to apply.

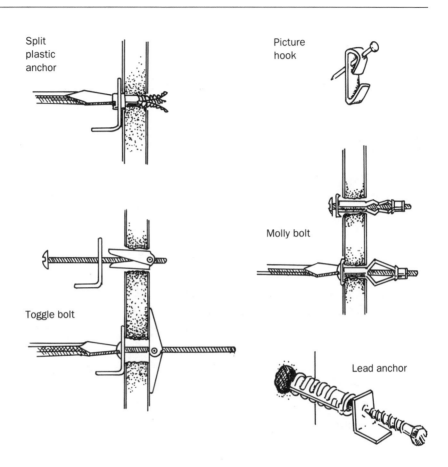

It won't have to if you use the right hardware to do the hanging. Most of today's homes have interior walls that are hollow. The framing is done with 2x4 studs, and then sheets of wallboard are nailed to the studs. Studs are generally located every 16 inches, and if you could nail into the stud for hanging, there'd be no problem. There are magnetic stud finders that locate the nails in the studs and, therefore, tell you exactly where the stud is. Usually, however, the stud isn't located where you want to hang Aunt Minnie's picture, so you have to hang it on the hollow part. Since the wallboard is usually sheet rock or gypsum board, this means that it has a core of something rigid but crumbly. Your nail will last only until the middle of the night when it will come out letting the picture fall and scare the liver out of you. With the proper hardware, your picture will stay.

For lightweight pictures, there are picture hooks similar to this one. The flat back plate of the hook is placed against the wall, and the nail is driven in at an angle. The angled nail and the flat plate distribute the weight, and the hook can hold up 100 pounds, depending on the size. A TIP: Place a tab of tape over the spot where any nail goes into the wall and prevent surface crumbling.

For mounting lightweight objects such as drapery hardware, use plastic wall anchors. They are sized according to the size screws you'll be using. The package they come in will tell you what size drill bit to use. When you've made the hole in the wall, tap the anchor into place. When the screw is installed into the anchor, the threads will push the anchor out against the sides of the hole causing it to grip tightly.

Shelves, mirrors, and heavier pictures usually do best with an expansion anchor commonly called a Molly bolt. Mollys come in different sizes according to the thickness of the wallboard and the weight to be held. The package will tell you what size drill bit to use. Tap the Molly shown into the hole so the two tiny teeth dig into the wall. Turn the screw head clockwise until it can't go any farther. This causes the expansion behind the wall as shown so the Molly is anchored. Now you can back out the bolt and attach whatever you'll be hanging.

Heavier objects such as cabinets, bookshelves, or a moose head require a toggle bolt. You must drill a hole to accommodate the flange while it is held closed against the bolt. The flange must open toward the hole when it's inside the wall. Also, once the toggle bolt is inside the wall, you can't remove the bolt part without the flange falling down behind the wall, so you must attach what you're hanging or its hook before installing the toggle bolt.

For mounting things on a concrete or masonry wall, there are lead anchors. A hole is drilled, and the anchor inserted. The bolt inserted does the same thing that happens with a plastic anchor in that the anchor expands against the walls of the hole to grip. There are all sorts and sizes of masonry anchors, and your hardware dealer will guide you into selecting the right one.

26

THIS DATE IN HISTORY

Back in 1870, the first part of the New York City subway system was opened. Before nightfall, all the subway cars had been painted with graffiti. If unwanted latex paint is on a surface with a different type of paint or finish, there are special products that will remove just the latex while having no effect on other finishes. Ask your paint dealer about these.

27

February may be the shortest month, but it is often the coldest. Think about keeping warm without using too much cold cash, but don't get caught with your plants down.

DON'T GIVE HOUSEPLANTS COLD FEET

In order to save on energy bills, many folks turn down the thermostat during these winter months. We should all do whatever we can to conserve energy, and once the body gets used to the slightly cooler temperature, we don't even notice it. If it starts to feel too cold, we can always turn up the electric blanket or wear warmer clothes. Here's another way to save. Unused rooms can be blocked off from the heat altogether.

Amid all this energy saving, what about those houseplants? Even though you brought all your plants in for the winter, they can still be damaged by the cold. Your philodendron can't slip a sweater on if the temperature is too cool, it won't turn blue, but it may start turning yellow around the leaves and even drop foliage. Most plants will be effected.

Protect your plants from cold damage by moving them into the rooms that are always going to be warm—the most used rooms. Keep them away from cold drafty windows. Move them away from exterior doors that are in regular use.

Also keep in mind that the thermostat measures the temperature of the air right where it is. If the plants are on the other side of the room and down on the floor, the temperature may be quite a few degrees different. Keep the plants as warm as possible and make changes as gradually as possible.

28

THIS DATE IN HISTORY

In 1858, the U.S. postal rate for first class mail jumped from 3¢ to 6¢. Now here's our 2¢ worth on buying a home.

HOT HOME BUYS

Many more homes are bought during the warmer months than during winter. It just might make sense because families don't like to move during the school term. Also nobody likes to walk through an empty house where the temperature is lower than your shoe size.

However, there may be advantages to winter looking, particularly if the house is in a colder climate. You get to see firsthand just how effective the heating system is. You can also see if there are cold spots in the house, and you can check around doors and windows to find out how much air infiltration you'd have to put up with. Also, if there's snow or ice around, you can see whether there are spots on the roof where the snow has melted. How did it melt? Probably a big heat loss from the house. You can look for icicles hanging from the gutters. This probably means clogged gutters. Not a big problem but if they've been clogged for some time, the water in the wrong place could have contributed to other problems.

You can also check the public transportation to see just how good it is in bad weather. Also, you can see what, if anything, the city does to keep the streets clear of snow or whatever Mother Nature has dished out.

Another big reason for off-season home shopping is that when there isn't much traffic through a house, and not very many prospects, you might find that the price is better and that the owner is a little more ready to haggle a bit on the price.

29

LEAP YEAR DAY

Every four years, in the years that can be divided evenly by four, it is a leap year—with an extra day in February. This extra day makes the calendar year equal to the solar year. There is another maneuver, the "leap second," that helps to adjust time so that atomic and astronomical time are coordinated. If you find that your Rolex is off by a second, this could be the answer.

MARCH

- *Again! It's filter time for the heating system.*
- *Check and clean the humidifier.*
- *Check and clean the screens in the hoses bringing water to the clothes washer.*
- *Run a gallon of vinegar through the automatic dishwasher.*
- *Prune away dead or broken limbs on trees.*
- *Inspect walks, drives, and other concrete structures for cracks and damage.*
- *Check and clean gutters and downspouts to get ready for April showers.*
- *Remove vent covers.*

1

THIS DATE IN HISTORY

In 1873, the first typewriter was manufactured . . . and here's a typewriter-related tip. A denture brush is great for cleaning the keys of a typewriter. The wider brush gets the job done faster than most conventional typewriter brushes.

It's also National Pig Day, but the denture brush might be a little slow for cleaning our swine friends.

2

In 1799, legislation was enacted to standardize weights and measures nationally. Measuring is a very important part of many home projects. There is an old handyman adage that says, "Measure once and you may cut twice. Measure twice and you'll only cut once." Since measurements aren't much good if you can't remember them, why not wrap a strip of masking tape around your rule to take notes on?

3

In 1931, the bill making "The Star Spangled Banner" our official national anthem was signed. Only three of the members of the

HOW TO REPAIR GUTTERS

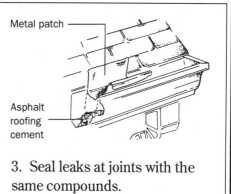

Metal patch

Asphalt roofing cement

Time to get ready for April showers.

1. Remove all rust and loose metal around holes. Use a wire brush and rust remover chemicals available at dealers.
2. Cover pinpoint holes with a dab of asphalt roofing cement or gutter sealer. Cover larger holes with a metal patch held in place by either of these compounds. Seal the edges from the top too.

3. Seal leaks at joints with the same compounds.
4. After the compound sets up, paint over the bare metal to seal against future rust and to make the patch blend into the rest of the gutter.

Senate and House who passed the bill could correctly sing the words to it. The words were written by Francis Scott Key in September 1814.

FLY YOUR FLAG! If mention of the National Anthem makes you feel patriotic, the rope on your flagpole will last longer if you'll coat it with linseed oil.

4

In 1881, James Garfield became the first U.S. president to use a telephone. If someone you're talking to on the telephone complains of static that you don't hear, sometimes you can rap the mouthpiece against the palm of your hand a few times. This may clear the air.

5

Emmett J. Culligan, a leader in the advancement of water treatment, was born on this day in 1893. The minerals in water are responsible for several appliance failures as well as plumbing problems. Lime and scale buildup can cut back on the efficiency of the water heater, stop the steam iron from steaming, foul the valve on the icemaker, and make water from the faucet slow to a trickle. If you can get to the mineral deposits, warm vinegar will usually dissolve them and get the thing working again.

6

In 1475, Michelangelo, probably the most famous ceiling painter, was born. If you're going to paint the ceiling, you'll probably end up with paint flecks all over your face. A thin coating of petroleum jelly will allow you to just wipe away the paint splatters.

7

In 1985, Victor Farris died. Before you say "Who?", he was the inventor of the paper milk carton. Every handyperson has used these containers for all sorts of home chores.

- These are good containers for soaking paint brushes.
- Fill the carton with charcoal briquettes and get your next cookout fire started quicker.

■ Keep one in the shop as a catch-all for small wood scraps. When full, it's a great starter for the fireplace.

8

THIS DATE IN HISTORY

In 1894, the State of New York became the first to license dogs.

If you have a new puppy, he'll sleep better and so will you if you provide a loud ticking clock next to his bed. The theory is that it makes him feel as if he has company and maybe he won't whine all night long. A hot water bottle wrapped in a t-shirt you just took off also helps. He gets the warmth of his mother and the friendly scent of his new pal.

9

A patent was issued for the first mailbox today in 1858. These roadside mailboxes seem to be invisible to heavy-footed drivers. Try wrapping the pole with reflector tape.

10

THIS DATE IN HISTORY

An unmanned Japanese spacecraft did a fly-by on Halley's Comet on this day in 1986. Studies were done on the comet's magnetic field, tests were made to determine the content of gases in the comet, and pictures were sent back to Earth.

MAKING SPACE FOR MORE STUFF

With spring cleaning coming up, there's an opportunity for you to get rid of a lot of things you have no use for. Why not do this with the all-American pastime, the garage sale! It's fun and can be profitable.

In deciding what to sell, be ruthless. Toss out *all* the things you don't need. Start in the attic and go all the way down to the basement. And don't skip the bookshelves, as books are big garage sale sellers. Books bring browsers so you have a constant crowd, which is desirable. Clothing does the same thing, and baby clothes are a big drawing card. Unless you're planning on more kids, that stuff should go.

Sporting goods, fishing tackle, and excess tools attract folks. Try to mention all these hot items in your ads, circulars, and signs.

If you don't have quite enough stuff for a big display, invite a neighbor or relative to join in the fun.

Price the stuff right and you may make enough to *hire* the spring cleaning next year.

11

On this day in 1818, a very important do-it-yourself book was first published. It was Mary Shelley's *Frankenstein*. The book did well, but making monsters at home never caught on with the public.

OLD HOUSE TIP

If your restoration project has a faulty masonry chimney, you can often install a metal flue in sections to go within the old chimney.

This leaves the authentic look without your having to make repairs to the old structure. The new flue will probably be safer, too.

12

THIS DATE IN HISTORY

In 1933, President Franklin Delano Roosevelt made his very first "Fireside Chat" broadcast on radio. It became a fairly regular Sunday evening thing.

13

THIS DATE IN HISTORY

The establishment of Standard Time in the United States was on this day in 1884. It was not formally established by Congress until March 19, 1918. This is typical of the speed with which government operates.

THE KOOKY CLOCK CAPER

The electric clock is the time teller most of us use at home. Most such clocks have a sealed mechanism so there's no way to work on one that starts to act up. However, if the clock has started making a whirring noise, try turning it upside down and letting it run for several hours. Doing this lets gravity redistribute the matter that has collected on the gears, which might stop the whirring.

14

Albert Einstein was born on this date in 1879. His mother claimed young Al was "sharp as a tack!" And . . . speaking of tacks, if you have to drive in these small fasteners and don't want to hit your thumb with the hammer, let a paper clip do the holding while you hold the other end of the clip, well away from the hammer blow.

15

It's National Buzzard Day. On this day every year, the buzzards return from their winter home in the Great Smokey Mountains to their summer home in Hinkley, Ohio. If buzzards or other feathered friends are devouring your young garden, artificial snakes coiled around in that area may spook the bird.

16 TREE STUMP REMOVAL

The best way to get rid of a tree stump in a hurry is to see if there is a firm that does stump-grinding. This process involves a machine that grinds the stump into wood chips. The grinder continues below the surface by several inches. Now the chips can be raked away and the area covered over with topsoil. As soon as the lawn takes root and covers the spot, the tree stump is just a memory.

17

It's St. Patrick's Day! Maybe you'd like to paint a room in your house green? If so, here are some thoughts on picking colors.

THE PSYCHOLOGY OF COLORS

Colors can have a profound effect on you and others in a room. So color selection before you start is very important.

For example, the color **red** on your walls could make you have increased muscular tension and actually even give you higher blood pressure. If, however, there's just a little red, it will be stimulating and warm.

Blue, on the other hand (or in the other room), can lower blood pressure, ease tensions, and make you more tranquil. Too much blue can sometimes be depressing.

The St.-Patrick's-Day **green** we mentioned is also restful, but if overused can become monotonous.

Yellow is great for keeping you at your peak efficiency and helping you stay bright and cheerful.

Purple gives a room a touch of pomp and stateliness, but some folks experience headaches from too much pompy purple.

Orange is a lot like red, but a too-orange room tends to physically tire people.

White gets the most from natural light but can cause eye strain.

Black is beautiful—but in small doses as background.

Gray is just a neutral color that does little for your emotional, physical, or visual senses, so it really needs accent colors to have any reason for being there.

Whether you believe in this color/mood business, it's a great excuse for you to procrastinate on starting the paint job.

18

George Washington Carver, the noted agricultural researcher who invented more than 300 products made from peanuts, was born into slavery and so his birth date is disputed. It has been said that he was born on this day, March 18, 1864.

Here's a use for peanuts that Carver might not have thought of. In shipping objects that need protection, use roasted peanuts still in the shell instead of conventional packing. The peanuts give pretty good protection and then the recipient can just eat the packing.

19

It's not as exotic as National Buzzard Day (March 15th), but the swallows return to San Juan Capistrano, California, on this day every year. Another way to keep the swallows or other birds away from the garden is to criss-cross strings over the area. Hang pairs of tin can lids from these strings. The breeze will cause the shiny lids to move and hit together. The movement and noise will keep birds away.

20

THIS DATE IN HISTORY

Uncle Tom's Cabin was first published on this day in 1852. When the weather is bad and you're stuck inside, you can develop "cabin fever." It doesn't have to happen. If you'll get into this do-it-yourself movement, you'll always have something to keep you occupied.

21

The first day of spring!!!

DOES SPRING BUG YOU?

When spring rolls around, we all end up working on lots of outside projects such as planting, mowing, painting, and the like. It's great to be working in the Great Outdoors . . . except isn't it amazing how many different bugs are out there to bug you? I don't mind an occasional buzzing attack, but some of these critters want to either bite or sting, and this I don't like. Thankfully, I have found a good insect repellent that works, but I've also learned that there are some things anyone can do to prevent being as much of an attraction for these pests.

First, avoid the use of cologne, after-shave, hair spray, or any scented cosmetics when you're outside. I'm not likely to be wearing makeup, but there are some folks who wouldn't show their faces outside without it. And, scents attract many insects, particularly bees and wasps.

Bright, colorful, and dark clothing also are more enticing to the insects. In fact, you may be a secondary target if you're working right next to someone wearing Chanel #5 and a loud Hawaiian shirt.

Finally, don't forget that the repellent effectiveness can be diminished by perspiration, water, and even wind. So give yourself another blast when needed.

Now, maybe you can enjoy the back-breaking work outdoors.

22

THIS DATE IN HISTORY

In 1987, a barge carrying 3,200 tons of garbage leaves Islip, New York. Its mission? Find a place to dump the garbage. The "gift" was declined by several states and foreign countries. Finally, after six months on the high seas, the garbage was returned to Islip.

Obviously, not too many people are fond of garbage but dogs seem to love it. If your garbage cans have been raided and the contents scattered over the yard, try putting the cans inside old tires. That way, the broad base makes it next to impossible for the dog to tip over the can.

Brush on a generous coating of black asphalt roofing compound on the bottom of the garbage can—inside and out—to prevent rusting out.

23

In 1699, John Bartram was born. He has been called the "Father of American Botany," and as such, must surely have shoveled his share of fertilizer. Modern day chemical fertilizers are considered better by many, if you can break the code.

Maybe the numbers on a bag of fertilizer confuse you . . . 5-10-5 or 20-10-10, or whatever. These numbers represent the percentage by weight of the three primary nutrients: nitrogen, phosphorous, and potassium.

Many gardeners have trouble remembering what each of those nutrients do and which number stands for which component. Here's the super easy way. Just remember the phrase, "Up, down, and all around."

The first number is for nitrogen and it does its thing "up" where you can see it by helping the lawn and other plants to grow. So if you want a greener, thicker lawn go for a fertilizer with a higher first number.

"Down" is for the middle number which is phosphorous. It helps root growth down below.

The third number is for "all around" and that's for potassium, which gives the plant all-around good health.

The phrase should help you to break the code, but be sure to ask the nurseryman what is the best fertilizer for your particular plant and problem . . . even if you have to look "up, down, and all around" to find him.

24

In 1912, twenty-five inches of snow fell on Kansas City. It may have been spring on the calendar, but somebody forgot to tell Mother Nature. When it's spring both on the calendar and in the sky, it's time for you to spring into action to fix what winter damage your home may have suffered.

- First, look for cracks and holes in outside masonry and brick work, including walks, drives, patios and the foundation.

- Inspect the roof for loose shingles. While you're up there, be sure the TV antenna is well anchored.

- Next, see that the gutters and downspouts are free and clear and have no leaks at the joints.

- Examine trees and shrubs for broken limbs. (And be careful that you don't get any broken limbs while climbing around up there.)

- Remove vent covers and check out the air-conditioning to be sure it's ready for summer.

However, don't let these things get in the way of the really important things, because spring is probably the best time to check out your swing on the golf course.

25

THIS DATE IN HISTORY

In 1775, George Washington planted some pecan trees that were a gift from Thomas Jefferson. March 25 is now known as Pecan Day.

When planting young trees, they often require stakes and wires to keep them straight during the early stages. The wires can cut through the bark and do damage. That old garden hose can come to the rescue. Run the wires through sections of the hose and position the hose pieces so they are where the wire would contact the tree. No damage!

26

The mowing machine was invented by Peter Gaillard in 1812. It was a far cry from the popular gasoline-powered mowers of today. With the mowing season just ahead, before you crank up your rotary mower, give it a quick inspection and get it ready for action.

First, remove the **spark plug.** With this out, you won't have any accidental starts while working under the **housing** . . . which is where you go next. Be sure the **blade** is sharp and balanced. If the blade is dull, remove it and use a file for sharpening. Be sure the blade is balanced before putting it back in: put a screwdriver shank through the center hole; the heavy side will go down. Keep filing it until the blade is balanced—or you'll get bad vibes.

Look at the underside of the housing for caked debris from last year. If you paint this area with drained crankcase oil from the car, grass clippings will be less likely to stick.

You're now ready to inspect and clean the **air filter.** Most are of the foam variety and can be cleaned with soap and water. Squeeze dry and add a few drops of light oil. Examine the condition of the **oil** and if it's okay, check the level. Clean the **carburetor** and be sure

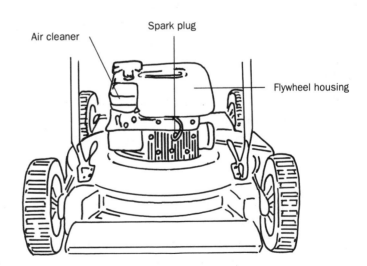

Air cleaner

Spark plug

Flywheel housing

the **choke** and **throttle** mechanisms are working. Lubricate all moving parts, including the **wheels.**

Finally, start with **new gasoline.** If you have some left over from last year, use it in your car or somewhere else. Otherwise, you'll gum up the mower.

Gentlemen, start your mowers!

27

In 1794, the U.S. Navy was started. Here's a hint for boat owners.

Have new "sailors" joined your crew? When rats take up quarters on your boat, it's usually because they've been able to walk along the mooring ropes. One possible solution is to put large funnels on the ropes, with the large open end facing the dock. Be sure not to put it too close to the dock, or the rats can jump over it.

28

That pesky volcano, Mt. St. Helens, erupted for the first time in this century in 1980. If you live near a volcano, the ash makes a great absorbant for lifting oil and grease spots out of concrete. Just cover the spots for twenty-four hours and when you sweep away the ash, the spot goes too.

29

The soft drink Coca-Cola was introduced back in 1886. Leftover cola is also the real thing at cleaning a toilet bowl. Just pour it into the bowl and let it sit for a while and the porcelain will sparkle.

30

In 1950, the invention of the transistor was announced. Without this step, millions of people wouldn't be walking around with tiny radios blasting their brains through headsets.

SAY WHAT???

The transistor radio gets the blame for an awful lot of hearing loss. But all noise, pleasant or not, can produce a certain amount of wear and tear on the old eardrums. Noise is a big part of our lives.

The home handyperson needs to be aware that the power tools that we enjoy and use often create a lot of racket. The chainsaw, circular saw, drills, routers—even a power mower—are all big offenders.

Many folks don't worry about these bursts of good honest noises but ear protection is a must. There are several different types of ear protection. Just having the gadgets won't help. You must make it a practice to always use them when you're running up the decibels. There's nothing you can do to reclaim the hearing loss from all your past fix-it projects, but you shouldn't make it get worse.

You hear me????

31

THIS DATE IN HISTORY

On this day in 1889, the Eiffel Tower was opened. Many people get dizzy when climbing to the top. After all, it's 984 feet tall. For climbing around the house, you should have a good sturdy ladder. Don't try to get by with a stack of books on a bar stool. That's an invitation to the emergency room. Inspect your ladder each time before you use it to be sure it's still in good shape.

Never paint a wooden ladder as the coating could hide cracks.

When getting high, play it safe!

APRIL

- *Filters!*

- *Drain the sediment off of the bottom of the water heater tank.*

- *Clean out the fireplace and check the flue for creosote build-up.*

- *Inspect the air conditioner to be sure it will be ready when summer hits.*

- *Get lawn and garden tools ready for action! Clean, oil, and sharpen!*

- *During an April shower, check gutters for leaks.*

- *When it's raining, walk all around the house looking for low places where water is puddling up. When the rain is gone bring in dirt to make the water drain away from the house.*

- *Examine roof for winter damage.*

1

APRIL FOOL'S DAY!

Was it an April Fool's Day Joke? In 1960, the U.S. launched its first weather satellite, but the weathercasters' accuracy didn't improve one bit.

These days, the weathercasters are telling us it's spring. Can the infamous spring cleaning be far behind? As you approach this task, keep safety in mind so you won't have to spring for a week in the hospital.

Many cleaning chores require the use of solvents, some of which are dangerous. Avoid the use of such dangerous solvents as gasoline, benzine, lacquer thinner, and others. In fact, when using any chemicals, including ordinary household cleaners, read the label for directions and caution notices.

Store oily cleaning rags, as well as oily work clothes or gloves, in an airtight metal container to prevent the start of a fire by spontaneous combustion.

Wear safety gear, including goggles, gloves, breathing masks, and whatever else is needed.

Many spring cleaning jobs require that you spring up high to get at the dirt. Never stand on a stack of books or a bar stool. Use only a good ladder.

Now maybe you can spring into action without doing damage to yourself.

2

READY, AIM, FIRE!!

In 1877, the first human being was fired from a cannon. What caliber of man would do such a foolish thing?

Spring cleaning is a time to examine a lot of stuff, including that Civil War cannon you never use. Or, the waffle iron your diet won't let you use. And the golf clubs you put away after that quadruple bogey on the front nine back in 1977. Or, the oversized Mexican sombrero you bought in Acapulco after six tequila shooters. Plus dozens of other things you keep packing away every year.

Let's face it, you don't want to give up these valuable parts of your life. If you're storing your relics in corrugated cardboard boxes in your attic, be aware that they aren't moisture-proof. Before taking the boxes up, give them a coat of thinned shellac. This not only makes them moisture-proof, but is added protection against rodent invasion.

3

Today is the birthday of Sally Rand, who invented the fan dance. She performed provocative dances by hiding her body parts behind a pair of feathered fans. She was born in 1904.

She may very well have started out with a pair of feather dusters. This old-time cleaning tool makes good sense.

TIP: Poke the feather duster handle into the end of the metal vacuum cleaner tube and you can reach up into high corners to get rid of cobwebs.

4

Probably the most famous ballroom dance instructor ever, Arthur Murray, was born on this day in 1895. If your dog's water bowl is dancing across the floor, put it on a rubber auto floor mat. This will also take care of spills.

5

PLAY IT SAFE

Last month (March 26), we got your mower ready to go. Anything that cuts that fast can be dangerous, so let's talk mower safety.

First, go over every inch of the lawn to pick up all the rocks, wire, toy cars, and other debris that could be picked up by the blade and thrown out with the velocity of a bullet from a .357 magnum.

Mowing is a lonely business so don't have an audience. They could get hurt.

Keep your hands and feet away from the blade at all times. Be particularly careful when starting the machine. Wear *closed* shoes.

Never refill the gas tank when the engine is running or even when it's still hot.

Turn off the engine when you have to leave it even for a moment.

Make certain you have good footing when mowing slopes or wet grass.

Make certain you know how to stop the engine in case of an emergency.

6

THIS DATE IN HISTORY

In 1965, the U.S. launched the first communications satellite, Earlybird. Ever since then, TV pictures have been fuzzy on cloudy days. Coincidence?

When installing a TV antenna, make sure to position it so that, if it should fall, it can't hit power lines on the way down.

7

In 1948, the first World Health Day was celebrated. Lawn mowing can be unhealthy to those with allergies. It may not be very comfortable but you'll breathe a lot easier if you wear a mask while mowing. People will say, "Who was that masked mowing man?"

8

FORE! Aerate your lawn as you mow each time by wearing your spiked golf shoes . . . and as long as you have 'em on, head for the course.

9

In 1971, an American Ping-Pong team went into the People's Republic of China. If your car is going "ping," it may need work, or you could try using a couple of tanks of higher-octane gasoline before taking it in for expensive repairs.

10

In 1872, the first Arbor Day was celebrated. It's a good day to go plant a tree. There's an old saying among arborists: "Don't plant a $5 tree in a 50¢ hole." This means that you'll ruin the tree if you don't dig a big enough hole . . . I think. (Where could you get a $5 tree these days? And nobody would dig a hole for 50¢.)

11

THIS DATE IN HISTORY

In 1894, twenty-eight inches of snow fell over several parts of the upper East Coast. Keep that fact in mind if you'd like to put off getting to all these chores we've suggested as possibilities for April. After all, it could happen again!

12

THE FAUNA IN YOUR FLORA

Don't get upset if your backyard has become a haven for frogs, toads, lizards, or snakes. These critters may be there because there are lots of insects feeding on the plants in the yard. These not-too-pretty creatures will help you fight the insects, so don't run them off.

There are also some insects that feed on other insects. The lady bug, the praying mantis, and the lacewing fly are all gardeners' friends. Most spiders that we see in the garden are also there to trap and devour insects.

While some birds will eat your crops, the purple martin is on a strict bug diet. How about putting up a martin house? These predators require no upkeep . . . just leave them alone and they'll do their thing with no damage to the ecology.

OLD HOUSE TIP

What's the first step in restoring an old house? Setting up a workshop. It's difficult not to actually go to work on beautifying the place, but having a complete shop will pay big dividends in ease of work and time saved.

13

APRIL IS GARAGE BEAUTIFICATION MONTH!

Isn't it time you did something about that crummy-looking area that you use so regularly? If you'll just think of the garage as another part of your home, you'll probably agree that it's the messiest room in the house. With a little effort, you can make your garage livable and more lovable.

Often the walls are not covered and have exposed studs. Applying sheetrock is inexpensive, easy to do, and can be a big help. This is a good training area for you to learn how to tape and bed. In the garage it doesn't have to be perfect. And this will look great on your resume.

And would you leave a room in your house unpainted? Why leave the garage bare? Painting won't take long. Maybe you can even use some of that leftover paint that's just taking up space.

Oil and grease spots are easy to clean up. And it wouldn't be the end of the world to sweep or vacuum the garage floor occasionally.

Mount or hang as much stuff as you can on the walls. It looks neater and there's not as much around for you to trip over.

Remember, the garage isn't just a place for things exiled from the house . . . that's what we have attics for!

14

In 1828, the very first edition of Webster's dictionary was published. Even if you don't know the meaning of "lovable" where the garage is concerned, at least you should want to make it more safe. For example, are there lawn and garden tools lurking around waiting to trip you? Some garages are so stuffed with junk that no normal-sized, slightly overweight person can walk through without a barked shin or a stubbed toe. And at night, if there isn't enough light, this annoyance becomes a regular mine field.

How about all those chemicals and insecticides: are they out where the kids can get into them? You should never have more than a small amount of gasoline stored, and even that can be dangerous if not in a proper container.

Even nondangerous things stored in a garage can become fire hazards. Like rags, clothing, or newspapers. Plus, these things offer havens for bugs and rodents.

Get rid of the booby traps in your garage today!

15

THE DREADED INCOME TAX FILING DAY

As you make improvements to your home, keep receipts. If you should ever sell the place, these costs can increase your investment in the house and therefore lower the profit from the sale. Your gain will then be less and so will the tax paid. (We're assuming you're going to make a profit . . . let's hope so.)

16

THIS DATE IN HISTORY

The "Fibber McGee and Molly" show premiered on radio in 1935. One of the show's gimmicks was McGee's closet. Each week he would open it and for several minutes you'd hear the sound of all sorts of things falling from the overcrowded closet.

Organizing your closets will not only make a closet avalanche less likely to happen, it'll help you to be able to store more stuff. Here are some ideas.

Stretch your closets without adding any space. Install a metal towel rack into the ceiling of a closet. Use toggle bolts to make sure it can hold some weight. Position the towel rack toward the rear of the closet. Now that you have a place for several additional hangers, make sure the new rack doesn't block your access to items on the regular closet rods.

17

In 1964, the first Mustang was introduced by the Ford Motor Company. Even if you don't own a classic, your car could probably stand a spring cleaning.

First, run the car through the automatic car wash to get off all the winter sludge. This will let you see the finish so you can look for any places where the paint has been chipped to expose bare metal.

Next, wash the underside to get rid of any chemicals that might have been used on icy roads. TIP: Positioning the lawn sprinkler at various points under the car may be just the ticket.

Inside, remove the floor mats and clean them outside the car. Sometimes, vacuuming will do. If they are vinyl mats, toss them into the clothes washer along with a coarse towel to do the scrubbing. If the mats are like carpets, use a carpet shampoo and carpet spot remover.

Upholstery should be vacuumed. Then it should be cleaned with whatever the owner's manual suggests. Vinyl will usually respond to any all-purpose cleaner but there are special vinyl cleaners available at auto supply stores. Fabrics can be treated like furniture. That means test any spot remover on an obscure spot before using it.

The clean car won't drive any better, but if it dies on the road, you'll at least have a pleasant place to wait for the tow truck.

18

THIS DATE IN HISTORY

In 1895, New York City opened the first public baths.

TIP: You wouldn't want to open your bath to the public if you have stains on the tub. Rust stains are fairly common on bathtubs. There are products at the supermarket for this problem but here's a homemade cure. Make a paste of cream of tartar and hydrogen peroxide. Smear this over the rust spots and leave it until it's completely dry. When you rinse away the dried paste, the rust spot goes, too.

19

In 1892, the first gasoline-powered auto was used in the U.S. If you run out of gas and a Good Samaritan comes along, but neither of you have a siphoning hose, use the hose from your windshield-washer system. After you're back in civilization, you can get it replaced.

20

This is a day of shame for paperhangers everywhere. In 1889, Adolf Hitler was born. When he bombed out in the wallpaper game, he turned to politics.

Wallpapering is definitely a do-it-yourself project. The first step in many cases is the removal of old wallpaper. There is no easy way . . . unless you have the strippable kind. Otherwise, the idea is to get water to penetrate the paper and this will tend to soften the paste underneath.

A good way to accomplish this is to use a large bucket of very hot water to which you've added some liquid detergent. The detergent acts as a wetting agent so the water sticks to the paper better. Apply the water with a paint roller and keep putting it on. When it soaks through, you can use a scraper to remove the paper. It usually is a slow process.

If the paper is vinyl, the water can't penetrate the surface. You must take a knife and make slashes all over the paper to admit water.

Steam is another way to go. You can rent a steamer, although there are newer models that are priced for the homeowner.

21

The creator of the idea of kindergarten, Friedrich Froebel, was born on this day in 1782. He believed that playtime was an important part of a child's education.

Whether your child is kindergarten age or younger, you should child-proof your home. Move all cleaning supplies, insecticides, and other chemicals that you have stored under the kitchen sink to a higher spot. Or, get a good child-proof latch for these cabinets. The same goes for the potions and lotions and cosmetics in the bathroom.

All stairways should have gates installed.

Electrical outlets that are low on the wall should have those plastic plug-in covers for the outlets not in use.

Small appliances with cords hanging down should be moved so the child can't tug and pull an appliance down on his or her head.

Take a tour throughout the house and grounds and look for all the things that could harm a child and either move them out of reach or lock them away.

22

THIS DATE IN HISTORY

The first Earth Day was celebrated on this day in 1967.

One of the problems with our planet is air pollution. Green plants and trees absorb lots of the pollutants in the air. At the same time that plants are removing poisonous gases from the air we breathe, they are replacing them with oxygen. So, instead of running around with picket signs, it might be better if we all started planting and growing more things so Mother Nature could take care of this problem.

23

In 1985, the Coca-Cola Company decided that their old formula wasn't the "real thing" after all. They introduced a new Coke which was, they said, the "real real thing," at least until July when they brought back the old formula and called it Coca-Cola Classic . . . really!

The bad thing about this and other soft drinks is that they come in cans that litter and plastic bottles that we can't seem to get rid of.

A good thing about the plastic bottles is that those 3-liter containers will act as mini-greenhouses for young plants. Just cut off the bottom of a bottle and place the bottomless container over the plant and it's protected from the sometimes too-chilly April weather.

24

YOU GET WHAT YOU PAY FOR

On this day in 1990, the $1.5-billion Hubble Space Telescope was put in orbit. It didn't work.

Without a telescope or even a pair of glasses, you can see that April showers make everything look fresh and green. It's a happy time . . . unless you try to drive your car through high water. While you should avoid high water, if you do encounter it, take it slow and easy so the fan doesn't spew water over the engine and maybe drown out the car.

If the water is deep enough to cover the tailpipe, the engine will probably be smothered to a stop. So avoid water this deep.

Also, test the brakes after fording the river as sometimes they don't work as well until dried out.

And before you venture out in the rain, be sure the windshield wiper blades work well.

25

THIS DATE IN HISTORY

In 1954, announcement was made of the invention of the first solar-powered battery.

Since spring is also planting time, you can use this to cut back on the solar power your home will be getting when summer comes. Landscaping can do a lot to help you conserve energy around the house.

A well-shaded home can be as much as 75% cooler on those real hot days.

Grass and other groundcovers can absorb heat that might otherwise be reflected toward your home.

Plant!

26

This is Richter Scale Day in honor of Charles Francis Richter. He devised the system by which we judge the magnitude of earthquakes. He was born on this day in 1900.

If you've put on a little weight during the dormant period, your patio chairs may let you go bursting through with a crash that could register a 4.0 on the Richter Scale. If they're the kind with plastic webbing, they may be easy to repair.

You can buy rolls of replacement webbing. First, though, you need to see how the old webbing is held in place. Some are held with screws, and if the holes have become enlarged, you may have to see if you can find a slightly larger screw that will work.

Others utilize clips that are also available where you buy webbing. The container in which you buy the clips will have installation instructions.

Wood-framed furniture may have the webbing held by tacks, screws, staples, or it may be sewn around the frame.

Not only will this easy chore make your patio less likely to experience an earthquake, the bright new webbing will certainly look better.

27

Today marks the birthday of Ulysses S. Grant, whose claim to fame is that he is thought to be buried in Grant's Tomb.

It's probably about time to entomb your woolens in the cedar closet until next fall. You should know that cedar odor does not kill moths. The odor does tend to repel them but there has to be significant cedar odor. If your cedar closet has lost this odor, often a light sanding of all the cedar surfaces will open the pores and again let the aroma come out. Also, vacuum the walls every year to prevent dust from stopping the scent.

If the closet door has spaces around it, weatherstrip to stop loss of the cedar smell. Also, all clothes should be cleaned before storage to ensure that no moth eggs are on them.

28

When spring rolls around, we take off the bulky winter clothes and discover the rolls of flab around the middle. Many folks drag out the ten-speed to try to pedal away the pounds.

Before you ride off into the sunset, however, do a few simple things to make certain the bike will make it back. Remember TLC. Sure, that stands for tender loving care, but in the bike game it stands for tightening, lubrication, and cleaning.

Tighten everything on the bike, paying particular attention to the seat and handlebars. Adjust the brakes and the gears and be sure they work properly.

Lubricate all the moving parts including the chain.

Now clean everything on the bike to be sure your hands or feet won't slip, and so the bike will look its best.

Check the tire pressure and have all the needed lights and reflectors if you'll be out after dark.

Just doing all that work will have burned off a few calories.

29

In 1968, the rock musical *Hair* opened in New York. If you just heard a chorus of flies buzzing the tune of "April Showers," you'll want to be sure that your screen door is free of holes. If you have to replace the screen on a wooden door, one key to a good job is making sure the screen is tight. By placing the screen on a long table top with a

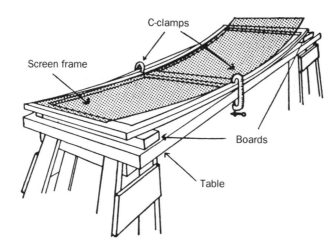

C-clamps

Screen frame

Boards

Table

2x4 on each end, you can use a C-clamp on each side to bow the frame in the center. Staple the new screen at each end and when you release the clamps, the screen will be tight as a drum. (See illustration.) Then staple the sides and cover the staples with molding.

With a metal door, there's a special, inexpensive tool called a "splining" tool that forces the flexible spline (thin plastic tubing) into a trough to pull the screen tight.

30

THE LAST APRIL SHOWER

From now on, you may have to use the garden hose to water the lawn, wash the car, and maybe even spray the kids on hot days. So why not get the hose out for a preseason inspection?

If everything looks okay, you're ready . . . until you run over the hose with your lawn mower. Then you end up spraying yourself through the slashes.

Before you throw the leaky thing away, you should be aware that most hoses can be mended. I'm not talking about wrapping a few turns of tape around because that remedy usually lasts only 10 hours and 4 minutes. Your lawn and garden dealer will have some nifty mender units that are easy to install after you've cut the bad parts out. (TIP: If you're working with plastic hose, hold the newly cut ends in hot water for a few moments until the plastic becomes more flexible and easier to work with.)

If you smashed the metal end pieces, there are also mender units for both ends of the hose.

Now, let us spray!

MAY

- *Don't forget the filters.*
- *Oil and inspect fans.*
- *Get the outdoor grill ready for the burgers.*
- *Time to get the patio furniture ready for some outdoor living.*
- *Clean and air out rugs and reverse them to spread traffic areas.*

1

It's May Day! In Russia, this is a big holiday for the working class. The old saying is, "A worker is only as good as his tools." In order to cope with the day-to-day home disasters, you don't need a lot of tools. Remember to buy quality tools. You'll do better with a good tool and it could last a lifetime.

ALL-PURPOSE TOOLS

HAMMER
Best all-purpose type is a carpenter's claw hammer and the 16-ounce size is good.

SAW
A cross-cut type will also cut with the grain.

SCREWDRIVER
Get a set that has several sizes and both regular and Phillips head tips.

PLIERS
Medium-sized slip-joint pliers let you get a grip on many problems.

ADJUSTABLE WRENCH
Get a 10-inch size. (Also called a Cresent wrench, which is actually the brand name for a popular brand.)

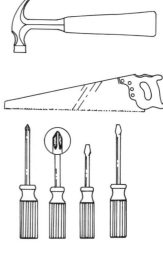

This will take the place of several wrenches, including metric.

UTILITY KNIFE

The type with a retractable blade is safer.

ELECTRIC DRILL
The only power tool for the basic list. Get a 3/8-inch drill with variable speed.

STAPLER
Select a bigger model than used in the office.

LEVEL
The pocket size will do fine.

RULE
A retractable metal rule that clips on a belt is handy.

FLASHLIGHT
Be sure to test the batteries from time to time.

PLUMBER'S FRIEND
The cup must be big enough to cover the kitchen sink drain opening.

ALSO . . . round out your tool kit with an assortment of nails, screws, nuts, and bolts, plus a roll of electrician's tape, a can of spray lube, and some all-purpose glue.

Keep all your tools together in a handy spot.

2

In 1939, New York Yankee first baseman Lou Gehrig missed his first game after 2,130 consecutive starts. He was called "Iron Man" because of this longevity. A handy friend is also called "Iron Man"— but because he uses an old ironing board as a work bench. He lives in an apartment and has no workshop.

3

THIS DATE IN HISTORY
In 1375 B.C., the first recorded eclipse of the sun occurred.

FUN PLANTS FOR JUNIOR GARDENERS

Hopefully an eclipse won't keep the kids from discovering the joys of gardening. Start your child on the garden path with some easy-to-grow plants that begin in the kitchen:

A citrus tree can be started from seeds from the next lemon, lime, orange, or grapefruit that you use. Save the fattest seeds. Wash them and let them soak in water overnight. Plant them about a half inch deep in potting soil. Space the seeds about an inch apart. Put the pot in a sunny spot and keep the soil slightly moist. It'll be a nice looking plant and if you're in for the long haul, you could have fruit in another eight to ten years.

The avocado seed can sprout into a fun plant. Give the pit a bath and then stick it with four toothpicks that will rest on the lip of a glass of water. The idea is to position the seed so about half of the rounded side is under water. Put the glass in filtered light and add water as it evaporates.

The top or crown of a pineapple can be placed in water and will root in a week or so. It can then be transplanted into a pot of sand to become a good-looking houseplant.

A sweet potato will take root in water and produce a nice looking vine. Put it in a container of water so that only half is under water. It needs sunlight and very shortly you'll start to see the roots growing.

4

THIS DAY IN BOONDOGGLE
In 1987, it was declared Tax Freedom Day. This meant that up until that date, everything that we had earned for the year was just enough to pay all our taxes. For the rest of the year, you were working for yourself . . . maybe.

Keep in mind that when you pay to have somebody perform some chore that you could do yourself, you're paying with dollars you've already paid tax on. In other words, you had to earn $1.28 or so to have that buck to pay. More reason to do it yourself and save!

5

THIS DAY IN SPACE
In 1961, Alan Shepard became the first American astronaut to go into space. You can help conquer your home space problems by making roll-out bins for storing things under the beds. This is a particularly good place to keep toys in a child's room.

6

In 1851, Yale patented the lock. Ever have a key break off in a lock? Often you can take a piece of a skinny coping saw blade and work it into the lock to grab hold of the key part. Why not examine your keys right now and have any bent key duplicated before it breaks off in your lock.

7

If your dog is chewing up his doghouse, make a paste of alum and water and smear this over the areas where he has chewed. He'll soon be broken of the habit . . . and maybe start chewing the legs of your Hepplewhite table.

8

It's Harry S Truman's birthday, and as a special treat on his birthday in 1945, the Germans signed an unconditional surrender.

Truman was one of the few haberdashers who made it to the White House. He had a very clever, handy use for an old necktie. When working in a dark area such as the attic, when you need both hands for the tools, tie a necktie over the top of your head and under your chin to hold your flashlight on your head. It looks stupid but it works.

9

HAPPY BIRTHDAY, MURPHY BROWN
Yes, in 1946, Candice Bergen was born. What do you do with those leftover, partly burned birthday candles? Keep a couple in a water-tight pill bottle along with a few kitchen matches. You'll have a sure-fire starter for the campout. Poke one into a small jar of petroleum jelly for an emergency light during a power failure. It will burn for hours!

10

In 1818, silversmith and alarmist Paul Revere died. He probably would have liked this weird way to clean silverware. Cover the bottom of a large glass dish with aluminum foil, shiny side up. Place the silverware in the dish and add a quart of hot water and a tablespoon of baking soda. Turn the silver once to clean both sides. If there is any protective coating on the silver, this doesn't work . . . otherwise, it's sort of unbelievable.

11

THIS DATE IN HISTORY
The first Polaroid camera went on sale in 1949. The handy person has found good use for these quick pix. One use is to have something to carry in when trying to get a replacement part for an appliance. Instead of using a technical term like "thingamajig" or "dodad," show the dealer a picture.

12

In 1971, there was a student protest over the cutting down of elm trees in Stockholm. In North America, the stately elm has been almost totally eliminated by Dutch elm disease and the plague of elm leaf beetles. Before planting any variety of elm tree, check with a local arborist to see how it will fare in your area.

13

In 1866, a horrendous sandstorm hit New Jersey, of all places. Many a home handyperson creates his own sandstorm in preparing for painting. You can contain much of the sanding dust in the room where the work is being done by hanging a plastic drop cloth over the doors leading to other rooms. Always wear breathing protection when sanding.

14

In 1878, Vaseline was trademarked. Since then, people have discovered hundreds of uses for petroleum jelly. Here are a few for the handyperson.

In fact, if you're handy or not, almost any chore you tackle can leave you with those yucky, dirty, grimy, grungy hands. Rub petroleum jelly into your palms and it forms a sort of invisible glove that makes it easier to just wipe away the mess from your hands. It also protects your face from paint platters when painting the ceiling.

Removing a nut and bolt from time to time will be an easier task if you smear petroleum jelly over their threads. It's also great for threads on an outdoor light bulb to prevent corrosion and to make removing the bulb easier. Another thread use is with the slip nuts that hold the sink trap to the drain under the sink. A thin film of petroleum jelly will seal the joint against water oozing out around the slip nuts.

A coat of petroleum jelly will also prevent rust from being able to attack metal parts and tools in storage.

15

In 1856, Lyman Frank Baum was born. He wrote *The Wizard of Oz* and made the Yellow Brick Road famous.

Brick roads, walks, and patios are easy to make without using any mortar. First, you need to dig out for a 3- to 4-inch bed of sand. This should be tamped down. Just place the bricks flat on the sand and as close together as possible. Be sure to use bricks that can handle weather and wear. It's probably a good idea to make a border from pressure-treated 2x4s to contain the bricks around the edges.

With all the bricks in place, sprinkle sand over the surface and sweep back and forth to get sand into the cracks between bricks.

Turn on the garden hose with the nozzle set to mist. This will soak the sand on down. When the surface is dry, repeat the sanding, sweeping, and misting until the cracks are filled with sand.

If there is ever a sinking area, just dig out the low bricks and pack in more sand before replacing.

Easy to build and easy to maintain . . . but the bricks don't have to be yellow!

16

THIS DATE IN HISTORY
In 1929, the first Oscars were awarded.

17

Graumann's Chinese Theater opened on this day in 1927. This is the place where they started the idea of stars signing their name and leaving hand prints in wet cement in front of the theater. Make your own family memory walk by pouring stepping stones. If you wish to have round stones, use a garbage can lid as your form. Let each family member sign, scratch in their birthday, and leave hand prints. You could also have extra steps for special days like anniversaries or the day the mortgage is paid off.

18

In 1949, the Antiquarian Booksellers Association was incorporated. Does this mean old people who sell books or people who sell old books?

As a personal aside, I have never been able to get rid of books. I still have books from college on courses that I didn't enjoy then and will never read again. I have also kept hundreds of paperbacks. Having all these books presents a storage problem. Some of the books have ended up with mildew as a result of poor storage. If you have mildewed books, sprinkle cornstarch on the effected pages and usually the mildew will soon go away. If you're going to store books, also place in a bag with newspaper to absorb moisture.

19

The first conviction using fingerprints as evidence occurred on this date in 1911. You can avoid leaving fingerprints on freshly polished brass by wearing rubber gloves during the polishing and until the brass is either sprayed with a protective coating or is back in place.

20

THIS DATE IN HISTORY

On this day in 1899, cabbie Jacob German, whizzing along in cab #1565, was given the first speeding ticket. It happened in New York City on Lexington Avenue, and Jacob was clocked at 12 mph. The patrolman who chased him down was on a bicycle.

If your bike is going to be left outside for a spell and there's a possibility of rain, slip a shower cap over the seat. When you're ready to roll, remove the shower cap and ride away on a dry seat.

21

The first bicycle appeared on the streets of Manhattan on this day in 1819. It was considered such a hazard that in a short while, the city fathers passed a law forbidding its use in public places and on sidewalks.

A bike storage idea is to use large screw hooks installed in the ceiling of your garage. Be sure the hooks go into joists or other solid wood. The bike hangs by the front wheel, up out of the way, taking up no floor space.

22

The Reno Gang pulled off the first Great Train Robbery on this date in 1868. It involved an Indianapolis-bound J-M & I train and occurred at Marshfield, Indiana. The haul amounted to about $98,000 and a conductor's railroad watch.

TIMER TIP

If your watch has been stolen, your radio can act as a timer. Most commercials are either a minute or thirty seconds, and they're usually almost to the second.

23

Ben Franklin is said to have invented bifocals on this day in 1785. If you wear your bifocals all the time, that snap-lid glass case makes a dandy container for drill bits.

24 On this day in 1899, the people of Boston discovered that parking was a problem and so the first parking garage was opened. If you have to park on the street, be sure not to leave packages or valuables inside that will tempt a thief.

25 Babe Ruth hit his last home run on this day back in 1935. It was number 714.

HINT OF THE DAY
Save an old broken baseball bat. The wood is usually ash and makes good stock for replacement chair rungs.

26 **HAPPY BIRTHDAY, PILGRIM**
It's John Wayne's date of birth and it happened in 1907. If you've retired your cowboy boots in memory of the Duke, put 'em to good use. Fill them with pebbles for weight and use each as a decorative door stop.

27 Feminists celebrate today as the birth date of Amelia Bloomer, an early woman's rights advocate. Yes, the feminine attire known as "bloomers" was named after her although she didn't actually create the style.

Old feminine attire can still be of service to the handy. The toe of an old nylon stocking can be slipped over the rim of a can to pour paint through for straining.

Twisted, a nylon stocking becomes very strong. Strong enough to tie into a loop and temporarily replace a broken fanbelt on a car. Strong enough to use as a tie-down when hauling bulky stuff.

28 This was a big day for the motion picture industry in 1929. It marked the release of the first talking picture made completely in color. Color certainly makes a difference in our lives, and not just in the movies.

If you're going to paint the exterior of your home, color selection is important because if you goof and pick a weird color, it's out where everybody can see it. What looks good on the little chip on the color card may turn out to look like a bad joke on the entire house.

One great way to select colors is to find a house with a color scheme you like. It should be a house with some similarities to yours and have somewhat the same ratio of siding to trim. Also consider roof color, any brick color, and even the colors on the houses on either side.

Some folks like the idea of taking a black and white photo and using water colors to see what the new color scheme might do. Or, trace the photo and use colored pencils. Neither will give you true colors, but either will give you an idea of the contrast between siding, trim and accent colors.

After you've decided, buy a quart of each color and actually paint a portion of the house. It'll look a lot different than the color card did. Enough so that you may want to change colors. Look at it in the shade and the sun to be sure.

If you like it, then you can paint the entire house.

29

OLD HOUSE TIP

In stripping paint in an older home, there is often the danger of old coats of paint being lead-based. There are test kits that tell you the presence of lead and then there are strippers that employ a plastic film applied over the chemicals so that all the paint is peeled away the next day along with the plastic. Play it safe where lead is concerned.

30

The first record of an automobile accident was recorded in New York City on this date in 1896. Henry Wells, driving his Duryea Motor Wagon, hit Evelyn Thomas, who was on her bicycle.

Bike safety is very important because if you have a confrontation with a car, tree, or brick wall, the bike will usually lose and the rider has very little protection.

Of course, you must obey all traffic laws. But one reason for accidents on a bike is the bike itself. Make sure the brakes are working properly. The chain, sprockets, and gears should be looked over. Check all the nuts and bolts that hold the handlebars and seat in place. Inspect the tires and wheels before each ride. Have the proper lights and reflectors for night riding.

Wear your helmet!

31

MAKE MY DAY!

It's Clint Eastwood's birthday.

As a final hint for the month of May, why not get your outdoor grill ready for summer fun? Look for and remove any rust spots. If repainting is called for, be sure to use a high-heat paint. Clean the grill surfaces using oven cleaner and a wire brush.

If it's a gas cooker, inspect all connections for leaks. You can use a soap mixture or that stuff the kids use to blow soap bubbles.

Enjoy!

JUNE

- *If you have central air, the filter routine continues year-round.*

- *Oil air conditioner blower fan.*

- *Inspect outside condenser/compressor unit to ensure a free flow of air through the fins.*

- *For window units, clean the filter.*

- *Consider turning off the pilot light to the furnaces.*

- *Be sure there are no dripping faucets to waste water.*

- *Inspect the septic tank if you have one.*

- *Clean the toilet tank.*

- *Move the houseplants outside for the season.*

1

THIS DATE IN HISTORY

The siesta was officially abolished in Mexico on this day in 1944. If you're looking for a place for your siestas, you can often create new space by converting a garage, attic, or basement into a living area.

An attached garage is ideal! There is already a floor and three of the four walls. A suspended ceiling is a great way to lower the existing ceiling and is an easy do-it-yourself effort.

Did you know that the average-size double garage can become a large family room or den, ideal for a siesta? Or, you might get two smallish bedrooms and a bath. But check the local building code as many have certain minimums as to the size of rooms. A rule of thumb: the National Code says all rooms except kitchens and bathrooms must have at least 70 square feet.

Other minimums are that a kitchen must have at least 50 square feet. Halls should be at least 3 feet wide. For an attic conversion, ceilings must be at lest 7 feet 6 inches for at least half the floor space and no lower than 5 feet at the lowest place.

If you end up with a too-small room, it may seem more like a cell, and who can siesta in jail?

2

On this day in 1835, P.T. Barnum's famed circus started its very first tour. Whether you have a circus tent or a small camp-out type, if you've ever had to sew on one, you've learned why the thimble was invented. When you need to sew on safari and don't have a thimble, just tape a coin to your index finger and you can push the needle through without hurting yourself.

3

THE MARRIAGE BED

In the olden days, the entire wedding party accompanied the bride and groom to their marriage bed. Probably the largest marriage bed ever made was completed on this date in 1430. It was for Phillip, Duke of Burgundy, and Princess Isabella of Portugal. The bed measured 19 feet by 12½ feet.

Since June is the traditional wedding month, here's a great idea for a bridal shower present. Go to your favorite hardware dealer and pick out a tool box and a set of the most-needed tools (*see May 1*). Paint the tool box white if you wish. This is sure better than toaster #11. If you select good tools, the set may last longer than the marriage.

4

HONK HONK!

The first Ford automobile was wheeled out of Henry's garage on June 4, 1896. Since then, millions of families have taken to the road for a vacation by car. Before you go, read about some checkups to make before you leave.

YOU AUTO CHECK THE CAR BEFORE YOU LEAVE

If you're going off on your annual family vacation by car, I'm sure you'll check the oil and gas before you leave. But that's not all you need to do. (*See also the safety inspection checklist on October 13.*)

- The coolant that we used to call antifreeze should be at the right level and at the proper concentration . . . usually 50%. If the coolant is a year old, you probably ought to change it.

- Check the wiper blades.

- Be sure all the lights and flashers work.

- All the car's vital fluids should be checked: brake fluid, power steering fluid, transmission fluid, and windshield washer liquid.

- Check all your engine's hoses and belts and replace if necessary.

- Look in the trunk to be certain the spare and jack are there.

- Maybe the most important check to make is on the tires. Every inch should be given a visual inspection to be certain that there is sufficient tread, no gouges or cuts, and no unusual wear that could indicate steering, balance, alignment, or suspension problems. Gauge the tire pressure, including the spare, and then put your tire gauge in the glove compartment so you can check the pressure daily while you're on the road.

Now, get the kids and the credit cards and enjoy!

5

The first safety deposit vault was introduced on this date in 1865. This proved to be a better hiding place than behind a loose brick in the fireplace. However, there are some good homemade "safes" that may fool most thieves.

My favorite is "the fake heating vent ploy." Most homes have hollow wall construction, which means framing is made with studs and then the wall is formed with sheetrock. You'll probably want to place the fake vent up high on the wall. Locate adjoining studs within the walls and cut a hole between the studs that can be covered by a vent cover. Vent covers are very inexpensive and come in various sizes. Install a 2x4 horizontally between the studs to act as a floor for your safe. Install the vent cover with screws and when you need to get inside, these fasteners will easily come out.

6

In 1876, bananas were introduced at the Centennial Exposition in Philadelphia. Some people swear by the use of bananas to control fleas in the yard. Banana peels are scattered in the yard at night. By the next morning, hundreds of fleas will have been attracted to the peels and the peels and pests can be picked up and placed in a plastic bag.

This may not be the cutting edge on flea control but it's certainly a good excuse to enjoy lots of banana splits!

BANANA TRIVIA
The largest recorded banana split was a mile-long concoction using almost 11,000 bananas and almost 33,000 scoops of ice cream! It was created in 1973 in St. Paul.

7

The first dog licensing began in England in 1735. This gives us an opportunity to give you a more scientific way to control fleas than yesterday's banana bit. The most effective way to control fleas is to attack on all three fronts at the same time: Treat the yard, the dog, and your home, all in the same day.

For the yard, there are many places that harbor fleas. These include tree trunks, shrubs, and the sides of buildings and fences. These have to be sprayed, so use a liquid and spray everything from the waist down. You have several choices of insecticides specified for fleas.

For the pet, be sure the product you select is specified as safe to use on the pet. Or, let the vet do it.

Inside the house, get an aerosol labeled for fleas in living quarters. Treat the whole house as well as the pet's abode.

For the best results, make three such treatments a week apart.

You should be aware that if your neighbors have pets and fleas, you can't be rid of the fleas on your property very long. It's great if you can get the entire block together and all treat the same day.

Also, the #1 carriers of fleas are rats and mice. If you have these critters, you have to get rid of 'em. (You should get rid of rodents even if you don't have a flea problem.)

Be sure to read and follow all the directions on the labels of all products used in the battle.

8

The first vacuum cleaner was introduced on this day in 1869. It was invented by Ives W. McGaffey and not J. Edgar Hoover as many folks think.

TIP: After sanding furniture, use a vacuum cleaner to remove most of the sanding dust. Then run a tack rag over the surface just before applying the new finish. *(See make-your-own-tack-rag instructions on June 26.)*

9

On this date in the year 128, Emperor Hadrian of Rome took some of the fun out of taking a bath. He decreed that the public baths in the empire could no longer be shared by men and women.

In modern times, soap scum on the tub also takes a lot of the fun out of bathing. One way to remove this stuff is with hot vinegar. Just apply with a sponge or rag and then use a scrub brush. Kerosene also does a number on soap scum deposits.

10

On this date in 1948, Chuck Yeager became the first human to go faster than the speed of sound. That's one way to escape the noises that bug us!

TIP! Most noises within the home have a way of getting into the bedroom when you're trying to nap. A lot of noise travels around doors because of the cracks around and under the door. The same weatherstripping that can stop cold air from coming in around entry doors can stop a lot of noise. Weatherstripping is inexpensive and easy to apply. You may be able to sleep better.

11

In 1947, the sugar rationing that was instituted during World War II was ended. How sweet it is!

TIP: Add a little sugar to such mixes as spackle or plaster of Paris to slow the setting time. This is a big help for us slow workers.

12

On this day in the year 1849, the gas mask was patented.

The day after a party, you may wake up wishing you had a gas mask. The aroma of smoke, beverages, and tuna fish tidbits does not give up easily. Place a dish with vinegar in it in each room where the odor is and after a couple of hours, your nose can breathe easy again. Or, if you have central air conditioning, even if it's not warm enough to turn it on, place a solid room deodorizer inside the return air vent and turn on the fan. This will send the good scents throughout the house.

13

In 1949, George Orwell's book *1984* was published. It was a look into the future. There's a way to look into the future in furniture refinishing. When you're ready to apply a finish to bare wood, wouldn't you like to know whether it's going to look the way you hope? Just take paint thinner on a rag and wipe it over about a square foot of the surface. While it's still wet, it will enhance the color and bring out the grain just about the same as a clear finish would. If it doesn't look quite right, now is the time to add stain, not after the real finish is applied. The paint thinner will evaporate rapidly, allowing you to finish your work.

14

Today is Flag Day! Why? Well, the first flag of the United States of America was adopted by the Continental Congress on this date in 1777. The first official celebration of Flag Day didn't happen until 1877 on the 100th anniversary of that adoption.

PUTTING UP A FLAGPOLE

Wouldn't this be a good day to put up a flagpole to show your patriotism? First, find out what restrictions there might be as to height and placement.

Next, shop around for flagpole units. Some have a sleeve that is set in concrete as a base for a pole that is put in and bolted in place. This is much easier to handle than having to deal with the long pole while the concrete is setting up.

The hole should be three times the diameter of the pole. The depth will be specified according to the type and length of the pole. Dig out an extra four to six inches and add a layer of small gravel for aid in drainage. After you've dug the basic hole, come back with a shovel and undercut so the hole is "belled" out at the bottom.

Premixed sacks of concrete will be the easiest. All you need do is add the prescribed amount of water. Pour in a couple of inches of the mix and then put in the pole or holder sleeve. Use a level or plumb bob to be sure the pole will be straight. If you didn't get the type with a sleeve, rig up braces to hold the pole in position until the concrete sets up. As you pour, use a stick to poke the mix to help work out any air bubbles.

Mound the concrete at the top so it's higher than the soil level to let rain drain away from the pole. After the concrete is cured, put a bead of caulk around the pole at the top of the concrete.

Now place your right hand over your heart and repeat after me, "I pledge allegiance to the flag of the United States of America and to the Republic for which it stands, one nation under God, indivisible, with liberty and justice for all."

15

This is supposed to be the actual day that Ben Franklin did his bit with the key and kite showing that lightning was actually electricity. It happened in 1752.

Lightning can do great damage to houses and their contents, particularly electronic things. If your home is the highest point around, you should investigate the possibility of having a lightning rod system installed to protect your home.

16

In 1941, the first federally owned and operated airport opened in Washington, D.C. Some say that the term "air sickness" came into being as a result.

Next time you fly, take a couple of the air sickness bags back home. They have a waterproof liner and can act as temporary paint brush storage bags for when you need to take a break. You don't have to clean the brush and it'll be ready to go when you come back.

17

The first clock dial was created by Jacopo Dondi on this day back in 1344. Time . . . or maybe lack of time . . . is a key ingredient in many successful do-it-yourself projects.

Never start out on a project unless you have time to finish it and do it right. You know there is usually going to be something unexpected that will happen, so leave yourself a little margin of extra time. And, if it's a project you've never done before, double that margin.

Even a simple paint job demands that you not stop in the middle of a wall or other surface because when you finally have time to come back and finish, you'll probably leave a streak where you left off. Be sure to leave enough time between coats for the previous one to dry before applying the next.

If you're too impatient and use something you've just glued before the adhesive has time to set up, it's liable to fall apart.

Many compounds require a certain time before they cure or set up. Jump the gun and they may not do what they're supposed to do.

Concrete that doesn't get the full curing time may not last.

Not waiting for a roof to dry after a rain can make your attempt at repairs a death-defying feat.

Time is often the key to success but it can also be used as an excuse to procrastinate. Use it when the time comes.

18

On this day in the year 1929, Richard Drew came up with the idea for cellophane tape. It was the forerunner of many other types of tape found in the home and workshop. Want a dandy dispenser for several different rolls of tape? An old wall-mounted toilet paper dispenser will serve you well in the shop. Mounted to the wall, the roller will hold several rolls of various types of tape side by side.

19

Back in 1910, this day was the first celebration of Father's Day. It may have come about because it was the day that many fathers got the bills from Mother's Day. Today would be a good day to make Dad and Mom and maybe Uncle Pete happy by getting rid of the oil spots on the concrete. This is an easy one. Saturate the spot with paint thinner. Before the paint thinner evaporates, cover it with a generous layer of an absorbant. You can use cat litter, corn meal, saw dust, or any powder that will absorb. When you sweep it up the next day, the spots will be gone.

20

THIS IS GREAT SEAL DAY!
This doesn't mean the kind of seal that clapped at its own tricks in vaudeville. In 1782, Charles Thompson submitted his report to Congress recommending the design for the Great Seal of the United States. This day also marks its adoption by the Congress.

It's possible that you'll adopt an even greater seal if you're building a deck. The wood, even if you use pressure-treated lumber, should be treated after completion. You should wait about thirty days before applying a water seal. You can do this job quickly by using a pump-up type garden sprayer. After the job is done, clean the sprayer by running some paint thinner through it.

21

In 1948, CBS/Columbia Records introduced the 33⅓ rpm LP record. Old phonograph records can become almost instant bookends. Use a handheld hair dryer to heat both sides along a line through the middle of the record. The heat makes it possible to bend the record. When you have it formed into an "L" shape, let it cool and you have a bookend.

22

HERE'S A REAL CORKER!
Although corks have been used as stoppers in bottles for centuries, the U.S. patent for a corkscrew was not issued until 1860. Makes you wonder how anybody enjoyed a sip of the grape before then.

One trick to use if you can't find your corkscrew is to install a screw eye into the cork. Then insert a screwdriver blade into the eye to use as a handle to pull out the cork. A stubborn cork may be coaxed out if you wrap a rag dipped in very hot water around the neck of the bottle. The glass will expand and let go of the cork.

23

On this day in 1868, three gentlemen from Milwaukee got a patent on the first typewriter. It was put on the market in 1874 by Remington & Sons, the gun makers. Maybe they thought that if the pen is mightier than the sword, the writing machine might be mightier than the .22 rifle? When you use a toothbrush to clean typewriter keys, dip it in kerosene, paint thinner, or lacquer thinner. Stubborn deposits can be removed from the keys with the point of a pin.

24

In 1948, Harry S Truman signed the draft act on this very date.

In the good old summertime a little bit of a draft can certainly help you stay a bit cooler without having to turn on the air conditioner. You might enlist a little help with the use of fans.

Ceiling fans are very popular. They not only help you keep your cool, but many are very decorative additions to the home.

Installing a ceiling fan in place of an existing light fixture in the ceiling is very simple because the electrical wiring is already there.

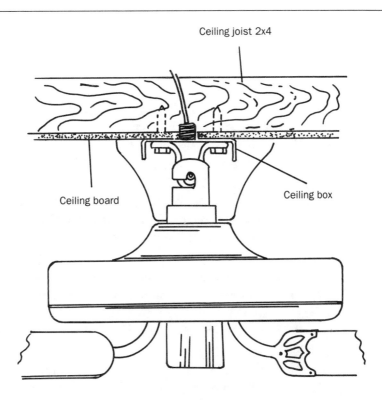

Ceiling joist 2x4

Ceiling board

Ceiling box

Be sure to go to the electrical entry box and shut off the power to the circuit on which you'll be working.

Since the fan is probably going to weigh considerably more than the light fixture, you must be sure the ceiling box can hold it. If the box has been installed in a notch in the ceiling joist, you can anchor the fan to that same joist. If not, and if you can get into the attic, you can nail a 2x4 between the joists and across the top of the ceiling box.

If you can't get into the attic, there are several different metal brace systems for ceiling fans. They go into a small opening in the ceiling and attach to the adjoining joists without your having to go into the attic.

25

THIS DATE IN HISTORY

In 1947, the first flying saucer was reported. Kenneth Arnold of Boise, Idaho, claims to have seen it over Mount Rainier, Washington. It was classified as a UFO.

Painting Outside

Exterior painting follows many of the same rules as interior painting (*see page 143*), but with some other preparation too.

1. Caulk around doors, windows, and other joints.
2. Repair and replace damaged wood.
3. Reset any loose nails.
4. Scrape all loose flaking paint.
5. Kill all mildew. Use a formula of ⅔ cup trisodium phosphate (TSP), ⅓ cup non-ammoniated powdered detergent, 1 quart liquid laundry bleach, and 3 quarts of water. Scrub the mildew spots, and then hose the surfaces clean.
6. Hose or scrub all surfaces to remove all dust or dirt.
7. Be sure the surfaces are dry before applying paint or primer.
8. Prime all bare wood with the primer suggested on the label of the top coat you have selected.
9. Be sure all previous coats are fully dry before adding subsequent coats.
10. Paint only when the weather is right: no rain in the forecast, humidity low to moderate, and mild temperatures. Plan so you don't paint in the direct sun if possible.
11. Be sure ladders and scaffolding are safe. If you don't have such, rent them.
12. Start at the top on the broad areas and work down. Do trim last.
13. If walks, drives or shrubs are in the way, cover them with tarps.

26 MAKE YOUR OWN TACK RAG

Dust is probably the biggest enemy you'll encounter in furniture refinishing. After you've applied the finish, and it has set up, any dust particles that were on the surface of the furniture before you started are now sealed in forever. Sometimes it can look pretty bad.

One of the keys to a better finish is to use a tack rag. These are inexpensive to buy in the paint store or paint department. However, making your own tack rags is an easy project and can save a little money, plus the fact it's not always convenient to leap into the car and go out for supplies when you're in your grungy refinishing clothes.

For the rag part, you need a well-washed lint-free cloth made of cotton. Leftover diapers are great. Old oxford cloth shirts are also good, but be sure you get rid of the buttons. Heavy cheesecloth is all right as is any other old piece of cotton cloth.

The first step is to cut the cloth into handkerchief size. If you use pinking shears to cut with, there's less likelihood of ravelling. Now dip the rag into lukewarm water and wring it out as completely as possible. Next, you must saturate the rag with turpentine. You can pour some turpentine into a bowl and dip the cloth in. Again, wring the devil out of the rag.

Since it's called a "tack rag," it's got to be tacky. This is done with varnish. Place the rag out on a flat clean surface and drip varnish all over the surface. Probably the easiest way to drip is to transfer some varnish into a clean empty plastic container with a cap in which you've punched a hole. Make the dots about every inch apart in an all-over pattern. Fold the cloth together so the dots face each other. Now roll it up and wring it and knead it to spread out the varnish. Unfold and refold in another direction. Wring and knead again. The idea here is to spread the tackiness so it coats the entire cloth uniformly. Keep up the wringing and rolling and folding until it is uniform.

Test it to see if it's right by running over a surface. The tack rag should be tacky enough to pick up dust and hold it, but should not leave the surface of the furniture with a tacky feel.

The time to use the tack rag is just before you start to apply the varnish or other finish. Work just a little bit ahead of the brushing.

When not in use, store your tack rags in a tightly sealed jar. If the rag needs restoration, add a few drops of warm water followed by drops or turpentine. Wring it out thoroughly.

Attack the dust with your tack rag, whether you make it or buy it, and your furniture finishing will have a better chance at success.

27

In 1917, the bill installing Daylight Saving Time was passed on this date. If you have trouble remembering which way to set your clock when these two times come around each year, it's "Spring forward and fall back." So in the spring you set the clocks forward an hour and in the fall you set them back an hour.

28

The first salt factory in America was founded on this date in 1630.

SALT

Nutritionists often tell us we use too much salt in our diets. Actually, handy people use salt around the house in many ways which certainly aren't harmful to your health. Maybe you've tried some of these uses.

- Salt sprinkled on a cutting board or butcher block can be rubbed with a lemon wedge to remove all sorts of stains in the wood.

- Soften up new denim work clothes by putting a half cup of salt in with the wash.

- Ice cream salt can be dissolved in water and poured in cracks in the concrete to prevent grass and weeds from growing there. Some people also flush ice cream salt down the commode to prevent tree roots from clogging the drain line.

- Soot on a carpet can be covered with salt; after an hour, both salt and soot can be vacuumed up.

OLD HOUSE TIP

Many very old houses may have calcimine paints inside. This stuff is almost impossible to paint over with latex because the calcimine is water soluble. The moisture in latex starts to dissolve the calcimine and your new paint peels. How do you tell if the old paint is calcimine? Use very hot water and start scrubbing. The calcimine paint will wash right off. If the paint is sound, you can often recoat it with oil-based paint. Otherwise, wash it all off. Add trisodium phosphate (TSP) to the water for faster removal.

- Cover spills in the oven with salt immediately. When the oven cools, the spill wipes up instead of being baked on for life.

29

In 1919, a Miss Belinda Bergan is reputed to have taken the first bubble bath—in a homemade version of the modern-day spa. The bubbles were made by sticking the hose of a handpowered tire pump into the water. No mention is made of the name of the pumper.

However, when such a pump loses its breath, it's often because the leather plunger inside has dried out. Often you can revive it by giving the leather a good shot of oil. Then go find someone who wants to take a bubble bath!

30

In 1949, the uranium boom was a big thing. A pocket-sized geiger counter was introduced that operated on flashlight batteries. When you can buy batteries at sale prices, keep the extras stored in the refrigerator until they are needed. They last a lot longer that way.

JULY

- *Do I have to remind you again about filters?*
- *Check the refrigerator for gasket leakage around the doors.*
- *Very important! Check the batteries and working order of smoke alarms.*

1

CAULKING

Caulking is important to your home because it can seal gaps that would allow moisture to get in and cause problems with building materials. Caulking also can button up air leaks that can cost you additional energy dollars. Sometimes caulking does nothing more than act as a cosmetic.

Where do you caulk? Usually anywhere you have two different parts of the house meeting you'll have a need for caulk. Like where door and window frames come together with the sides of the house. Or, where the side of the house meets the foundation.

Any place where two different types of building materials meet is also a likely caulking candidate. Like where the concrete steps or porch meet the house. Or where the chimney meets the roof. Caulking is also used where plumbing pipes go through a wall and where exhaust vents come through.

There are lots of different types of caulks and your dealer can make sure you get the right type for each chore.

The actual application of caulk is easy. Remove all the old caulk and clean the surfaces to rid them of dirt, dust, wax, oil, or whatever. Take your caulk gun and cut the tapered spout at an angle and at a spot that will give you the right size bead for the gap at hand. Hold the gun at about a 45-degree angle in the direction of your movement.

2

On this day in 1945, the blackout in England was lifted and the lights went on for the first time since September 1939. Some of your lights probably don't work. If your favorite lamp won't come on until you jump twice on a certain spot on the floor while holding your mouth a certain way, this is probably an easy repair. And with the lamp *unplugged,* it'll be a safe repair, too.

First check over the plug and cord for visible flaws.

If the problem isn't there, you may wish to replace the socket. It's a very inexpensive and easy replacement:

1. Remove the bulb. The top outer brass shell separates from the base by merely pressing in on the top part where the two sections

104

join. When loose, this brass shell slides off, revealing a cardboard sleeve which slides up, revealing the socket. You can then see the two wires. Check to be sure they are properly connected. If so, loosen the screws and disconnect the wires. You can usually use the old base.

2. If the wires are frayed, snip off the ends and strip the insulation back about ¾ inch. Twist the strands so, in effect, you create two solid wires. Curl these to fit around the screws in a clockwise direction. As each screw is turned it will pull the wire tighter around.

3. Be sure there are no strands of wire sticking out and that the two wires don't touch each other.

4. Now put the insulating cardboard sleeve back on, followed by the brass shell. Snap it back in place and plug the lamp in. With any luck at all, you should have light . . . without any stomping.

3

The first passenger car manufactured in the United States since February 1942 rolled off the assembly line at the Ford Motor Company on this day in 1945. The assembly lines as well as steel and other materials had gone into the war effort. Tires were also a scarcity.

Today's tires are made to last longer but lots of people don't get the full mileage from their tires. Underinflation is a really big reason for this. You should check your tire pressure at least every week. A tire pressure gauge is inexpensive and every car should have one.

When is the best time to check tire pressure? When the car has been idle long enough for the air inside to be completely cool.

Do this regularly and you'll have a safer ride, plus the tires should last right up until the warranty expires.

4

IT'S INDEPENDENCE DAY! Today we celebrate the signing of the Declaration of Independence by the Continental Congress back on July 4, 1776. Let this patriotic holiday also remind you of the fact that you can declare your independence from the repair man if you learn to do it yourself.

★ Today is a good day to check the batteries in your smoke alarm. (*See December 30.*)

5

GRIN AND BARE IT

On this date in 1946, the bikini made its public debut at a fashion show in Paris. This was a shot in the arm for the tanning cream industry, what with all that extra skin being exposed.

Besides sunburn, there's another problem with too much exposure to the sun . . . wrinkled skin. Did you know that if you paint the exterior of your home in the sun while wearing your bikini, you're inviting wrinkles for you . . . and your new paint job?

Nobody wants a wrinkled house!

What happens is that the top layer of paint dries faster than the part underneath and wrinkles occur.

If you want to paint during the summer, plan the job so you'll actually be applying the paint in the shade. Start the morning on the north or west side and follow the sun. Don't work so fast that you catch the sun or so slow it catches you. And don't start so early that the surface is still wet with dew.

After you finish the paint job, you've earned your place in the sun to bag some rays out by the pool.

6

THIS DATE IN HISTORY

In 1954, Elvis cut his first record. At the time, some said it was more noise than music.

Noise is something we often have to live with around our homes. Some noises can be very frightening. Like when the refrigerator starts to make noise, you can become afraid that you'll have to buy a new one. Actually, there are several not too serious reasons for weird noises from the refrigerator.

One very common noise maker is a vase or something on top of the unit that is rattled by the vibration. That same vibration can cause the pan underneath to shake, rattle, and make noise. It can cause the water supply tube to the icemaker to bang against something.

There is a fan inside the freezing compartment and another underneath the unit. If the set screw holding the blade onto the shaft is loose, the blade can propel itself forward and hit something. A bent fan blade can also cause this problem.

The compressor is on rubber mounts to absorb shock waves when the unit runs. If these mounts get loose or harden, you'll hear a strange noise.

The mere fact that the box isn't level can also cause it to make strange sounds.

7

The first comic magazine in the United States was published on this day in 1802. It was edited by Robert Rusticoat, whose nickname was Rusty Turncoat. It was called *The Wasp*.

There's nothing comic about wasp stings, so if you see nests around the house, get rid of them. There are wasp and hornet sprays that shoot a stream about twenty feet. The best time to attack is at dusk because all the wasps will be back home and disoriented by the dark. Spray and then run like crazy. You'll kill all that the spray hits and any that escape will not come back to that nest.

If you see a wasp inside your house, spritz him with hair spray!

8

Back in 1907, Flo Ziegfeld staged his first Follies. It occurred on the roof of the New York Theatre.

A lot of folks think it's folly to get up on a roof, but now is a good time to make sure your roof is ready in case a troop of dancing girls show up. You can inspect the roof without actually getting up there.

Drag out the binoculars to help you spot trouble spots at ground level.

A trip to the attic will allow you to inspect the underside. Also, look for water stains on the rafters. Or, better still, go up during a rainstorm and actually see where water may be coming in.

Be aware that if you call a roofer to make repairs, many will automatically tell you that you need a new roof instead of just a few repairs. Get a second opinion . . . and a second estimate.

9

A STITCH IN TIME

Elias Howe, inventor of the sewing machine, was born on this date in 1819.

HANDY TIP: If the foot pedal to your sewing machine creeps across the floor, attach strips of peel-n-stick weatherstripping to the bottom. The foam will make it slip-proof.

10

SINK OR SWIM? The first life preserver to ever be approved by the Board of Supervising Inspectors was the Neversink Cork Jacket invented by David Kahnweiler and patented on this day in 1877.

Did you know that in an emergency, the spare tire from your trunk—even with the weight of the wheel—could be a life preserver? Most full-size spares will float. But be sure that in tossing it to a person in trouble that your aim is good enough to miss the victim.

11

The first commercial production of plywood in the United States was started on this date in 1905. It was made by the Portland Manufacturing Company of Portland, Oregon. You'll have less splintering when cutting plywood if you run a strip of masking tape along the intended cut line. Then saw right through the tape.

12

PAPER OR PLASTIC? The first paper bag manufacturing machine was invented by Bill Goodale and was granted a patent on this date in the year 1869.

Paper bags find lots of extra uses around the home. Instead of buying wrapping paper for mailing packages, cut and flatten grocery sacks.

Collect small wood scraps and shavings and put them in small paper bags to use as firestarters in the fireplace.

You can light up your walk or driveway with paper bags half filled with sand. Insert a candle in the sand and light it. The sand acts as ballast for the bag and also extinguishes the candle when it burns down that far.

13 THIS DATE IN HISTORY

French revolutionary writer Jean Paul Marat was murdered by girlfriend Charlotte Corday in 1793. It happened while he was in his bathtub.

The bathtub can be a dangerous place even without a murderous friend. Slippery tubs account for lots of injuries from falls. That's why those nonslip stick-on strips are so popular. The adhesive really holds. So when you decide to replace the strips in favor of a different color, it's very difficult to get them to let go.

The people at Rubbermaid, who make more of those appliqués than probably any other company, recommend that you use a prewash spray such as Spray n' Wash or Shout. Just spray around the edges of all the strips and let that sit for about thirty minutes. Then use a single edge razor blade held flat against the tub so as not to scratch. This allows you to get the strips loose to peel up. Then spray again to remove any adhesive that is left. After another thirty minutes, a coarse towel will get rid of this stuff.

Don't forget to replace the strips so you don't fall.

14

MEASURE UP! The first patent on a tape measure was granted to Alvin J. Fellows on this date in 1868. It was the forerunner of the kind so many handy people wear on a belt. The tape was encased and had a spring click lock to hold the tape at the desired place.

Your retractable rule will work better if you extend it all the way out and then let it retract through folded-over waxed paper. Wear a glove while doing this so the metal tape can't cut your hand. The tiny amount of wax that rubs off will keep the rule working smoother.

15 ST. SWITHIN'S DAY

You might say it was coincidence, but the reason some people celebrate this day was because it rained like crazy on the day St. Swithin's remains were moved from the yard outside into Winchester Cathedral. It continued to rain for forty days. Saint Swithin had been dead for 109 years but his fans gave him credit for having performed a miracle from the beyond. That was on this date in 971.

According to some in England, any time that it rains on this day, the wet stuff will continue to fall for forty days. If the day is fair, there'll be no rain for forty days.

If the next St. Swithin's Day is fair, your umbrella can still be useful. As you mist your plants, hold the open bumbershoot behind the plants to protect the walls as you spray.

16

THE BIG TOP BITES THE DUST

In 1956, Ringling Brothers Barnum and Bailey Circus folded its tent and the next season began appearing in air-conditioned arenas. When camping out, most of us have spent some happy times in a tent. It's not as convenient as home but it's got a certain charm. Your tent home can be better organized with a few handy pockets on the inside walls. Of course you can sew pockets on but unless you have an industrial-strength sewing machine, working on heavy canvas isn't all that easy. That iron-mending tape meant for use on denims is an easy way to add the pockets made of scrap canvas or even worn-out jeans. Vary the sizes and you'll have holders for all sorts of items.

17

THE WRONG STUFF

On this day in 1938, Douglas "Wrong-Way" Corrigan left New York to fly to California. He ended up in Ireland instead.

This sort of reminds me of a lot of do-it-yourselfers who start out on a project without knowing which way to go. Then when things are hopelessly fouled up, they decide to read the directions.

Make sure you read the directions all the way through *before* you start. If you just read step 1, do what it says, and then go on a step at a time, you'll find that step 9 says, "If you live in the North American continent, skip step 3 or the whole project explodes." Before you start, be sure you understand all the steps, have the procedure in mind, and know the sequence of events. Also see that you have all the necessary tools and materials.

Another big reason for reading all the labels and instructions is to find out about dangers and safety directions.

If you've read everything several times and realize you still don't understand it, it's probably a sign that this project isn't for you.

The old Air Force slogan, "When in doubt, read the directions," really applies . . . and you should start each project with a little doubt in your heart.

18

If you're superstitious, you may wish to stay clear of Rome on this, the day on which the city burned twice. It happened once in the year 390 B.C. and again in A.D. 64.

No matter where you are, you should know that the kitchen is a common room for house fires to start in. If you're not careful, you could burn more than the toast. Here are some safety rules for the kitchen.

Many folks head to the kitchen in the morning with a robe on. Many robes have loose flowing sleeves. Be sure not to let a sleeve touch a burner or trail across a flame or you could find yourself ablaze. Don't use a dish towel to remove a pan from the oven. The loose ends can catch on fire.

Don't store frequently used spices and condiments above the stove, where careless reaching for them could result in clothing catching on fire.

When frying, keep the lid handy, as it can smother out a grease fire. Also, grease popping out can burn you. Steam can also burn you without a flame. When removing the lid from a pan or hot dish, lift the far side first so steam or splatters go away from you.

When cooking, don't let handles stick out toward the front or you could bump the handle and flip a hot omelet out on your feet.

In case you don't follow all the safety rules, have an all-purpose fire extinguisher on hand and know how to use it.

19

The first American publication that qualifies as a newspaper was called *Publick Occurrences Both Foreign and Domestick*. Its first edition appeared in Boston on this date in 1690.

Newspapers have many uses after the "occurrences" have been read.

A crumpled wad of newspaper is the best window polisher that you can find after washing the panes.

Newspapers make great mulch for flower beds. Lay them out around plants and put a thin layer of dirt over the top. When watered, the paper will hold moisture. This mulch will deter the growth of weeds.

Stuff crumpled wads of newspaper into wet boots and shoes to absorb the moisture. This trick also works as a deodorizer. Try it also in musty trunks and to remove odors from a refrigerator.

And don't forget the bottom of the birdcage!

20

REAL MAN IN THE MOON

On July 20, 1969, Neil Armstrong became the first man to set foot on the moon. He and Edwin "Buzz" Aldrin landed the lunar module Eagle and Neil won the toss and climbed down first.

What would an almanac be without some moon facts?

For example, the diameter of the moon is 2,160 miles. If you were to plop it down on top of the United States and line up one edge with San Francisco, the other edge would hit the outskirts of Cleveland.

The moon's average distance from the earth is 238,856 miles.

The moon's trip around the earth takes 29 days, 12 hours, 44 minutes, and 2.8 seconds.

Because of the moon's rotation, we earthlings always see the same side of the moon.

It's a fact that you'll have bad luck if you look at a new moon over your left shoulder.

Another fact is that the moon is made of green cheese, in spite of the so-called moon rocks our astronauts have brought back.

21

OLD HOUSE TIP

Marble was a popular choice in older homes. If this material doesn't have the sheen it should, try automobile rubbing compound to regain the luster.

22

To foil foreclosure, the Federal Home Loan Bank Board was installed on this date in 1932. Homeowners who could not obtain private money for refinancing could apply here.

Did you know that the most expensive home-related item is not the lot itself, and not even your stereo sound system? In most cases, it's the interest on your home loan. Even though it's spread over a long period of time, this expense will usually more than double the amount spent on the house.

23

In 1965, a bill was signed eliminating silver from dimes and quarters. Precious metals were just too precious for us common folk to be carrying around in our pockets.

We do know how to take care of silver at home, however, and most folks keep their silverware clean and polished. If you have trouble polishing the edges of tines on forks, here's a tip. Use a piece of string coated with silver polish. Loop it around a tine and move the loop up and down for easy cleaning.

24

In 1969, an Englishman, John Fairfax, became the first person to row completely across the Atlantic Ocean alone. That's a lot of hard work! It would probably be even harder if the water in the Atlantic was what we call hard water.

We hear a lot of talk in commercials about hard water and soft water. You're probably saying, "Water is just water, so what difference does it make?"

Well, "hard" water can form more mineral deposits inside plumbing and water-using appliances. These deposits can cause damage and problems. You see, hard water has a lot more minerals than "soft" water.

Soft water has very little calcium and magnesium salts and it doesn't allow soap to suds very well.

Although there is no actual dividing line between the two, you're generally better off with water that is not very hard. There's not a lot you can do about it without getting a water treatment system, but there is an old farmer's way to tell if you have hard or soft water. Just look at your ice cubes. Hard water cubes have a whitish spot in the center where the minerals collect. Soft water cubes are uniformly cloudy all the way through. Almost everybody will see some white spots in their cubes because most city water is moderately hard.

25 **RING AROUND THE COLLAR!** Walter Hunt made a bold fashion statement when he received a patent on the paper collar. It was varnished to withstand perspiration and the ring could be wiped away with a damp cloth. It happened on this day in 1854.

Enough coats of varnish will make just about anything waterproof. I once saw a bathroom with all the fixtures covered with wallpaper. This included inside the toilet bowl, bathtub, and lavatory. A waterproof adhesive was used. Then, the creative homeowner applied 4 coats of marine varnish over the paper. The fixtures looked great and were completely functional.

26 **YOU AXED FOR IT!** The first U.S. company to manufacture axes opened on this day in 1800 in Johnstown, New York. It was founded by William Mann.

A good way to protect your axe blade in storage as well as preventing it from slicing a finger is to put a strip of slit garden hose over the sharp edge or edges and use a couple of large rubber bands to hold the hose in place.

27 A swarm of grasshoppers descended on large parts of the states of Iowa, Nebraska, and South Dakota on this date in 1931.

To the fisherman, this represented an opportunity because grasshoppers are pretty good bait. Live grasshoppers are best but even those that you can collect from the grill of the car have been known to lure some big ones.

28 It is said that on this day in 1867, Arm & Hammer baking soda came into being. If you wonder what the raised muscular arm and hammer symbol have to do with baking soda, the answer is nothing at all. That symbol was used by the Vulcan Spice Mill owned by James A. Church. It was borrowed from the Roman god, Vulcan. When Church shut down the mill and went into the soda business with his father, he took the symbol along. At one point, an effort to tie the

114

symbol to the product was made with the slogan that the product had the "force" to make dough rise.

BAKING SODA

Baking soda is a very handy product to have around the house, even if you never bake.

- Baking soda is a good nonscratching cleaner that can safely be used on plastic, plastic laminates, fiberglass, vinyl, stainless steel, chrome, and other household materials. Just sprinkle it on a damp sponge and then rub, rinse, and dry.

- We all know the trick of an open box of soda in the refrigerator to absorb odors. That used soda will still clean and deodorize the sink drain or disposer. Just pour it in and follow with 2 cups of boiling water.

- In the coffee pot use soda instead of coffee. Add the water and let the pot go through a brewing cycle. This takes away the bitter taste and also cleans stains in the pot.

- Put a layer of soda in each auto ashtray for a better smelling car.

- Keep a box handy to snuff out grease fires in the kitchen.

Baking soda has the "force" to do lots of other things around the home.

29

TV TRIVIA

On this date in 1957, Jack Paar became the host of the *Tonight Show*. Today's viewers who are used to hearing all sorts of four-letter words on the tube will find it hard to believe that in Paar's time, he was "bleeped" for using the initials "W.C." on the air. "W.C." stood for water closet, a more proper name for the toilet. He walked off the set the next day in protest. We've certainly come a long, long way, baby!

At the risk of running afoul of the censors, I want to discuss a common W.C. problem: the constantly running toilet. This may turn out to be a simple repair.

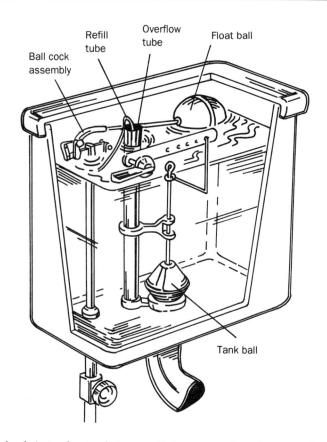

First, look into the tank to see if the water is going out through the overflow tube. This is an open pipe that sticks up in the center of the tank. If so, it may be a problem with the float ball.

This is a hollow ball on the right side as you look in. The floating ball stays atop the water until the tank is flushed, and then, with no water to keep it afloat, it drops down. As it drops, the rod to which the ball is attached moves and opens the valve on the other side of the tank to let new water come in.

At about the same time, the stopperlike ball or flapper drops back in place to close the opening in the bottom of the tank. As the tank fills, the float rises and the rod should move and shut off the flow of water.

If you see the water going out through the open pipe, lift up on the rod. If this causes the water to stop coming in, you know the float needs to be positioned so it shuts off the water at a slightly lower level in the tank. Grasp the rod with both hands, and with your thumbs together, gently bend the rod down on both sides from your thumbs. If that doesn't quite do it, try again.

If lifting the rod doesn't shut off the water inlet valve, your problem is in the valve itself. To take it apart, you must shut off the water supply using the handle under the tank. Turn clockwise.

Now you can take the valve apart and look at the washers and/or "O" rings to see what the problem is. These are inexpensive replacement parts.

If, when you look inside, the water level isn't above the overflow tube, it means the water is seeping out around the stopper. It may be a flapper type or the kind with lift wires as shown. If the stopper isn't falling back into the hole, you may need to reposition it. The stopper may be damaged and, if so, it's an inexpensive replacement part.

The opening may have a slight buildup of mineral deposits which would prevent a good seal. This can be removed with wet/dry sandpaper. There is also a repair kit that has a flapper attached to a metal ring plus waterproof glue to attach the unit.

Now your W.C. should be OK.

30

It was on this day back in 1975 that Jimmy Hoffa disappeared. No trace of him has ever been found. Some rumors suggest there was an excess of concrete from some project and that maybe someone made Jimmy a pair of concrete shoes.

Actually, any time you have a concrete project, you're liable to have a little left over. What do you do with the stuff? Well, if you don't have some alternate projects on hand, it will turn into a blob and you'll be wondering what to do with it. Then suddenly you'll know. You get out the sledgehammer and chisel and start chipping.

Stepping stones are a good alternate and you can usually find use for a few extras. Just have a rough wooden frame ready in case you have leftover mix. Include a coat hanger or two or chicken wire in the form as reinforcing metal. Coat the form with drained motor oil for easier removal.

31

The very first patent granted by the United States government was issued on this day in 1790 to a gentleman named Samuel Hopkins. It was for a process for making potash. Potash is used in making soap.

While you could make potash at home, if you're going to try your hand at soapmaking, there is an easier way. Go to the supermarket and get a can of lye to use instead of the potash. Here is one method of making light and gentle soap.

SOAP

Here are the utensils you'll need:

> 2 gallon kettle (*Cannot* be aluminum)
> 1 small pan to hold 6 pints of grease
> 1 wooden spoon
> Cup or ladle for dipping grease

The ingredients include:

> 6 pints bacon grease
> 2½ pints water
> 1⅓ ounce can of lye
> 1 cup 20-Mule Team Borax

Heat the grease in the small pan to melt it, but don't let it get beyond lukewarm.

Pour 2½ pints of water into the big kettle and then the can of lye. Lye is caustic and throws off harmful fumes, so treat it with care.

Add the grease slowly, stirring with the wooden spoon as you do. Add 1 cup of 20-Mule Team Borax. (Do not use any borax product that has additives.)

Stir gently every 15 minutes until the mix reaches the consistency of sour cream.

Mix in colorants and scents and pour into molds. Cover with a wet towel and place in a warm, dark location. Let the soap season for 3 weeks.

Cut the soap into usable bars and enjoy!

NOTE: Remember that you're dealing with harmful ingredients, so exercise care.

AUGUST

- *Guess what? Filters!*
- *Get the fireplace ready for fall. Check the mortar joints.*
- *Inspect and clean the chimney.*
- *Check the TV antenna to be sure you're ready for football season.*

1

The first roller skates were invented on this day in 1753 by a Hollander named Hans deFluken when he attached wooden wheels to his wooden shoes. Although ice skating was big in Holland, the new warm weather substitute didn't catch on at that time. Now, with the new "in-line" skates, the older style of skates have lost favor. However, if you have an old pair, take them apart and you'll have four pairs of wheels. Attach these to a sturdy rectangular board and you have a dandy dolly for hauling heavy things. It becomes even handier if you add a rope for pulling.

2

ROMANTIC MEALS

There's an old saying, "A dinner without candlelight is like a kiss without a mustache." (Author's note: I bring that up whenever I can since I have a mustache.) The first candle factory in America came into being on this day in 1748. It was in Newport, Rhode Island and was established by Benjamin Crabb. Unfortunately, the place burned down in 1750. (During a candlelight dinner?)

Candles are helpful for things other than "mood" lighting. Candle wax is a good lubricant. Rub a candle stub over a saw blade to protect the metal and also make cutting easier. A coat of wax on a metal saw table makes the work easier and protects the metal from rust. Wooden drawers operate more smoothly when the contact points are rubbed with wax.

When sharpening a saw blade, let a lighted candle leave a coat of soot along the teeth. Then you'll know which teeth you've filed. Drip candle wax on the end of a frayed rope to stop the problem.

And here's a new "mood" use. Put several candles in the fireplace on a hot August night. You'll have the warm look of a fire without the heat. But leave the candle stubs around to help start the real fire when cooler weather rolls around.

3

On this date in 1903, the Timberlake Wire & Novelty Company of Jackson, Michigan marketed their first wire coat hanger. Their primary product until then had been wire frames for lampshades. The hanger was created by one of their employees who got tired of his coat getting wrinkled because there weren't enough hooks for all employees to hang their coats. He took some of the scrap wire and hand-fashioned what we now have as a wire hanger.

Wire hangers seem to multiply in the closet. We'll have to do something about this or we'll be taken over by the hangers. There are some home uses for those extra hangers.

Pull out the center of the horizontal piece to form a rough circle. Dip the loop into a large container holding a mix of liquid detergent and water to which you've added a couple of ounces of glycerin. As you pull your loop gently through the air, you'll make giant bubbles.

For campouts, form a similar but smaller loop and cover the opening with aluminum foil. You have a good frying pan that can be tossed when the cooking is done.

Substitute netting for the foil and you have a net for catching minnows or butterflies.

4

FORTY WHACKS!

Lizzie Borden was arrested on this day in 1892 in Fall River, Massachusetts and was charged with the axe murders of her mother and stepfather.

If you'll be using your axe for a more normal reason, it's important to keep it properly sharpened. This can be done with a file but is best accomplished with a special round stone called a woodman's stone or combination axe stone. This stone has a coarse side and a fine side. To sharpen an axe or hatchet, move the stone in a circular fashion along the blade, starting with the coarse side and finishing with the fine side. A properly sharpened tool won't need anywhere near as many whacks to get the job done.

5

Primarily because of the oil crisis, the Department of Energy Organization was created by President Jimmy Carter on this date in 1977. It was headed by James R. Schlesinger. By October of that year the DEO had over 20,000 employees and Schlesinger had been given cabinet status. The DEO has yet to create the first quart of oil.

Instead of continuing to wait for the government to help, maybe if you know how energy dollars are spent in the average home, you'll figure out ways to help solve your own energy crisis.

Heating and cooling	58%
Water Heating	13%
Lighting	10%
Refrigeration	7%
Cooking	6%
All other appliances	6%

In some homes, as much as 66% of all energy consumed is wasted. That should give you something to think about.

6

THE HOT SEAT

The first execution of a human being by electrocution in the electric chair was that of William Kemmler, alias John Hart, in 1890.

Unfortunately, too many people are accidentally electrocuted around the home. When you're working on an electrical repair and have shut off the power to the circuit you're working on, it's a good idea to leave a note at the entry box to warn everyone not to restore power by flipping the switch. It'll only take an extra minute.

7

OLD HOUSE TIP

Leveling an ancient home is probably best done by a pro, but if you're adventurous, do the leveling very gradually. Sudden changes could damage other parts of the structure. Spread the force of jacks with 2x10's or even heavier timbers that run at right angles to the floor joists. The jack must be on a footing to prevent it from sinking into the ground instead of raising the house. Then when you raise the jacks, bring them up until they just touch the wood. Then make no more than a quarter turn per day.

8

THIS DATE IN HISTORY

In 1988, people with very little to do were excited that this date was 8/8/88.

On this same day in 1786, the decimal system of money standards was established and the dollar was made the basic unit. Congress also established that the smallest coin would be the "copper," 200 of which would equal one dollar.

Copper is a much more valuable metal these days. It's the metal of choice for much of the water supply lines in homes. Copper pipes are often joined by a method called "sweat soldering." Some think it is so called because you have to sweat out whether the joint will hold or not. It's really fairly easy to do but many homeowners shy away from it.

Most of this kind of soldering is done with a propane torch, using a paste-type flux and a solid core wire solder.

The surfaces of the pipe and the fitting must be made shiny clean wherever the two pieces are to join together. The shining is most often done with an emery cloth. There are special wire brushes for getting inside small fittings.

With the flux applied to these surfaces, fit them together and play the flame only on the copper, not the solder. When the copper is hot enough to melt the solder, remove the flame and touch the solder to the metal at the joint. As if by magic, the molten solder will be sucked into the joint.

Use copper pipe scraps and fittings for a practice session and you'll see just how easy it is.

9

OOPS!

For only $1.5 billion (that would be 300 billion coppers), NASA was able to get the Hubble space telescope. They should have spent a little more to get one that worked. The telescope was flawed because of a 1mm measuring error in the spacing in an optic device. The fact that there was a problem was discovered on this day in 1990.

Measuring is important to many of our projects around the house. But measuring goes beyond rulers, tapes, and yardsticks. The next time you're in a good big hardware store or home center, look at some of the other tools.

There are a number of squares available, the most popular types are the carpenter's square, the try-square, and the combination square.

The level and plumb-bob are also very helpful in many home projects.

Some of the newer tools have digital readouts, electronics, and maybe even built-in stereo. But still, the most common reason for a mistake in measurement is human error. If you can stand another old saying, "He cut off the board again but it was still too short."

10

The first Inspector of Milk in the United States was appointed in Boston, Massachusetts on this day in 1859.

REMOVING MILK PAINT

Back in those days, milk was often used to make paint, also called casein paint. It was a tough, almost impossible coating to remove. In fact, if you've stripped an old piece of furniture and the bottom coat of paint doesn't respond to your paint and varnish remover, it's probably milk paint.

There is a way to remove it. Household ammonia, straight from the bottle, can be rubbed on with steel wool and usually the paint will come off. Have plenty of ventilation to minimize the ammonia fumes and wear your rubber gloves. Keep the surface wet and keep rubbing because it takes time and effort.

Ammonia tends to darken some wood so you may have to bleach.

11

Henry S. Parmelee of New Haven, Connecticut got tired of hand watering his lawn so he invented the first sprinkler head. He was granted a patent for this in 1874.

If you don't have a sprinkler system in your yard, why not install one? It's definitely a do-it-yourself venture in many cases. The materials involved are fairly inexpensive and yet, having it done is somewhat costly. The biggest part of the expense is labor. By doing it yourself, you will save all the labor costs.

Many retailers that sell the materials for an automatic sprinkler system offer free layout and planning service. This layout will show you where each sprinkler head should go and what type head is needed to water the area. The dealer will also be able to tell you what water pressure is needed and whether any permits are required. He can also guide you on the depth at which the pipes should be installed.

A trenching machine can be rented but if the soil is right and if you have a spirit of adventure and if you dig digging, you can do this by hand.

PVC plastic pipe is the most widely used for sprinkler systems and it is super simple to install. If the system is of the automatic type, the wiring is very basic and very safe.

When the system is in, you'll enjoy the easy way of watering.

12

GOTTA LIGHT?

The friction match, often referred to as a "wooden kitchen match," was said to have been invented by an Englishman in 1827. The first of these to be manufactured in the United States was introduced on this day in 1834 in Chicopee, Massachusetts. They were made by Daniel Chapin and Alonzo Phillips. Matches can be made waterproof by soaking the heads in linseed oil for a short while. Wipe the excess away and when the oil is dry, the matches are waterproof.

13

The Master of Suspense, Alfred Hitchcock, was born in London on August 13, 1899. Among his thriller movies was *Rear Window*. Whether it's your rear window or front window, they're going to need repairs one of these days.

HOW TO REPLACE WINDOW PANES

1. Wear gloves. Carefully remove all the broken glass. Wiggle the shards of glass back and forth.
2. Remove all old putty. Use a wire brush and scraper. Hardened putty can be softened by painting it with linseed oil or by applying heat. The heat from a propane torch can work, but you must be careful. Heat lamps, heat guns, hair dryers, or a solder iron are

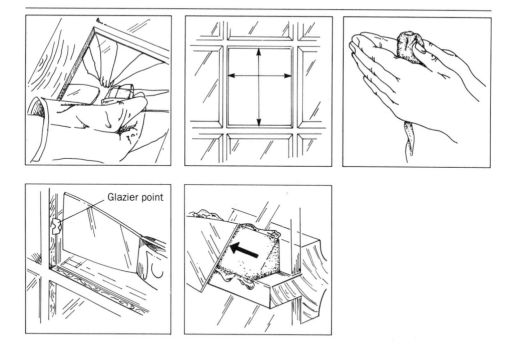

Glazier point

safer. Look for metal points in a wood frame and spring clips in a metal frame, and save these.

3. Measure both horizontally and vertically, and then subtract about a sixteenth of an inch to compensate for a frame that may not be exactly square. If the frame has a wide lip, subtract one-eighth inch. Recheck your measurements.

4. When you are having the glass cut to size, also pick up a can of glazier's compound or putty, and if you don't have the metal points or spring clips, get a box.

5. If the frame is wood, brush a thin coat of boiled linseed oil where wood and putty will come in contact.

6. Take a blob of the compound or putty and roll it between your hands to form a string about the diameter of a skinny pencil. From outside the window, press this against the window frame where the glass is to be placed.

7. Press the pane against the bed of putty until there are no air pockets in the putty.

8. Insert the glazier's points in a wood frame or the spring clips in a metal frame to hold the glass in place until exterior putty is in place. The points need only be barely pushed into place. For a

small pane, place them about six inches apart on each side. For big pieces of glass, also put them along the top and bottom.

9. Now place blobs of the putty around the outside of the pane and use a putty knife to bevel this bed to match all the other windows.

10. Remove excess putty from both outside and in.

11. Paint the putty after it's cured for about three days.

14

WHAT'S WATT?

A patent was granted on the electric meter on August 14, 1888. It was invented by Oliver Shallenberger.

Many people curse the meter because they relate it to the bill they get each month. Actually, it's a very fair way to measure the amount of electricity you use. If you wish to pay less, you need only use less. You have complete control!

READING YOUR ELECTRIC METER

Your power company bills you for the number of kilowatt-hours you use. A kilowatt-hour (kwh) is the use of 1000 watts for one hour. Reading the meter is a simple process. By taking the readings on a monthly basis, you can see what your usage is and maybe figure out how to cut back.

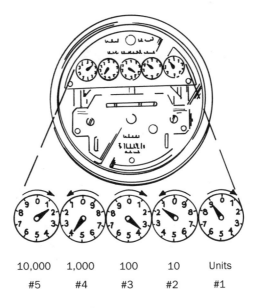

10,000	1,000	100	10	Units
#5	#4	#3	#2	#1

Most meters have 4 or 5 dials. The one on the far right measures 1 to 10 kwh. Dial #2 measures 10 to 100 kwh and the third dial, 100 to 1000 kwh. The 4th dial is 1000 to 10,000 kwh, and if there's a 5th dial, it measures 10,000 to 100,000 kwh.

Start at the right and move left. If the pointer is between two numbers, write down the lower number. If it's directly on the number, look at the dial to the right of it and see if the pointer has passed zero. You see, the dial to the right must make a complete revolution before the pointer on the next dial moves up a number.

Once you have the reading, subtract the previous month's total from it and you have the usage for the month.

Your readings cannot be exactly the same as the power company's unless you take the readings at the exact same time. However, if there is a large discrepancy, you can have them test the meter, which most power companies do on a regular basis anyway.

15

On August 15, 1961, the East Germans started construction of the Berlin Wall. If you'll be building a concrete wall—probably on a smaller scale—it can go up faster if you use concrete blocks on a concrete footing.

Also, instead of mixing up the mortar, you can buy 80-pound bags of a premix where all you have to do is add water. Each 80-pound bag will yield enough mortar mix to lay 27 standard concrete blocks with a 3/8" thick mortar joint.

HOW TO PATCH MORTAR JOINTS

Missing or cracked mortar joints between bricks are repaired with a process called tuck pointing. Here's the procedure:

1. Using hammer, chisel, and safety goggles, remove all material down to a depth of at least a half inch.

2. Hose out the cavity.

3. The easiest method is to use a patching compound in a cartridge for use with a caulking gun. However, this doesn't match the rest of the old mortar and may call attention to the patch. To more closely match the old mortar joints, use a dry mortar mix that requires only the addition of water. Follow directions as to the amount of water. Put a small amount of a trial mix on a piece of corrugated board to find out if it will match the old. The corrugated board will absorb moisture from the trial mix quickly so you can get a good idea of what shade the cured joints will be. There are powdered mortar colors you can buy, or you can use blackboard chalk dust to color or shade with. If the mix needs more darkening, use lampblack powder. When the trial mix is the same as the old mortar, you now know what shade to make the wet mix.

4. Dampen the joints, but leave no standing water.

5. Force the mortar into the joint with a trowel, filling vertical joints first. Press the trowel against the new mortar to be sure to eliminate any spaces.

6. Before the mortar sets up, rake the joint to make it match the configuration of the rest of the wall.

For a loose brick:

1. Remove it and chip away all the surrounding mortar.

2. Hose out the cavity and have it and the brick damp for replacing.

3. Lay a bed of mortar into the cavity.

4. Butter the top and ends of the brick with mortar.

5. Ease the brick into place using the trowel to push mortar back into the cavity.

6. Clean away the excess, and rake the joints as above.

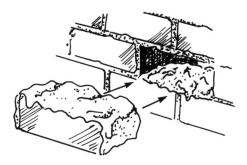

16

THE KING IS DEAD? At 3:30 P.M. on this day in 1977, Elvis Presley was pronounced dead. However, he was last seen three weeks ago in a hardware store in Baton Rouge, Louisiana in the process of buying some refractory cement.

Elvis, this is a good idea because it's not too long before you and Priscilla could be sitting before a romantic fire in the fireplace. But if there's mortar missing between the brick, you could have a fire hazard.

Refractory cement, also called fireplace cement, is the only kind to use. Common mortar mix won't hold up under the heat. Refractory cement will actually get stronger from the heat. It comes in small quantities and all you need to do is add water and mix.

17

MEANWHILE, BACK AT THE WRENCH
The first wrench patent in the United States was obtained on this day in 1835 by Solyman Merrick of Springfield, Massachusetts.

In olden days, a saber scar across the face as a result of a duel was sort of a badge of honor. To some, skinned knuckles are considered the same symbol to the home handyperson. However, if the skinned knuckles are from the use of a wrench, it probably didn't have to happen.

First, you need to have the right wrench for a proper fit for it to be able to have a good grip on the nut. A cheap wrench will often wear and lose its bite. A dirty wrench can make you lose your grip, as can greasy hands.

If you pull on the wrench instead of pushing, you're less likely to hit something with your knuckles if there's a slip. If you have to push, do so with the palm of your hand without closing your fingers around the wrench.

Most wrench accidents are caused by the nut on your end of the wrench.

18

A STICKY SITUATION
The first glue factory in the United States was established in Boston on this date in 1807. The company was founded by Roger Upton and

the glues were all made of animal products. Older horses would go miles out of the way to avoid passing the factory.

Although some animal glues are still being used, there are many new adhesives that do a better job. This glue chart may help you to decide which type of glue to use the next time someone tells you to stick it.

STICK-IT THE SUPER HANDYMAN'S ADHESIVE GUIDE									
TYPE	TYPICAL USES	FORM	APPLICATION	HOLDING POWER	WATER RESISTANCE	FLEXIBILITY	SET TIME	CURE TIME	SOLVENT
Contact Cement	plastic laminates, veneers	liquid	brush, roller, trowel	G	E	R	on contact	30–48 hrs	Acetone
Epoxy	almost anything	2 components mixed	stick, brush	E	E	R	depends on brand 5 min– 12 hrs	24 hrs	Acetone
Hide Glue	wood	flake or liquid	brush, stick	G	P	R	8 hrs	8 hrs	warm water
Hot Melt	wood, ceramics, leather, fabrics	melt sticks	electric glue gun	P	E	FLX	1–2 min	1–2 min	Acetone
Instant (Cyano-acrylates)	rubber, plastics (some), metal	liquid (tubes)	from tube	E	E	R	few seconds	1–12 hrs	lighter fluid, Acetone
Latex	carpet, canvas, paper	liquid	from tube or stick, from can	P	P	FLX	1–6 hrs	10–60 hrs	warm water, lighter fluid
Liquid Solder	metal (not electrical connections)	liquid	from tube	E	E	FLX	8 hrs	12 hrs	Acetone
Mastics	ceiling tiles, paneling, ceramic tiles	caulk paste	from caulk gun or with trowel	G	G	FLX to R	1–2 hrs	24+ hrs	Mineral Spirits, Turpentine
Polyvinyl PVA-White Glue	wood, hardboard, paper	liquid	from container spout	G	P	SR	1–5 hrs	24 hrs	warm soapy water
Resourcinol	wood	2 parts powder & liquid	brush, stick	E	E	R	7–10 hrs	24 hrs	cool water

The best source of information on any glue as to uses, setting, and curing time or clean-up is the manufacturer's information on the label.

G-good
E-excellent
P-poor
R-rigid
FLX-flexible
SR-semirigid

19

WESTWARD HO

The *New York Herald* published a story in their edition of August 19, 1848 telling of the discovery of gold in California. However, the big gold rush made by the so-called 49ers didn't happen until the next year.

Some furniture and picture frames have a gold finish called gilding. The easiest way to do this yourself is with powders, using a dusting process called bronzing. Large art supply stores and some hobby shops have supplies for this work and may even have literature on how it's done.

The best of these finishes is done with gold leaf. Very, very thin sheets of gold are applied to a tacky varnish finish. This is an old art-form, but supplies are available through outlets catering to the furniture refinisher. There are some woodworker catalog houses that have gold leaf, too.

While the process is too lengthy for these pages, it's not an impossible craft to learn . . . and is kind of fun.

20

BRUSH AFTER EVERY MEAL

On August 20, 1770, William Addis finished serving his prison term and carried out with him his new invention, a toothbrush. Until then, teeth were cleaned with a rag, if at all. Addis used a bone for the handle and installed stiff bristles in holes he had drilled. The toothbrush was a big hit and Addis cleaned up.

Old toothbrushes are a big hit with the handy-person. Here are but a few of the many uses.

- The small brush is great for all sorts of cleaning chores in tight places . . . like under faucet handles or in between heavily carved areas of furniture.

- This is an ideal brush for cleaning the grout between tiles.

- Dipped in a solvent, the toothbrush does a number on oily grime in hard-to-reach places around a motor.

- Handyman hands and yucky fingernails come clean quicker after a little work with a toothbrush.

- Those little specks used in some furniture refinishing are done with a technique called "spatter-dashing." The toothbrush and a popsicle stick will create the specks.

21

Although venetian blinds had been around for many years, the first patent was awarded to John Hampson on this day in 1841. It covered the creation of a way that allowed the slats to stay in any position they were set in. Did you ever wash venetian blinds and find that they had shrunk so much that they no longer could hook onto the bottom brackets? The simple solution is to put them back in place while the tapes are still damp.

22

HAPPY SOAP DAY! This was a big day in the history of soap. In 1830, Jessie Oakley introduced the first bars of soap that were individually wrapped. Also, liquid soap was first patented on this day in 1865, the bright idea of William Sheppard of New York City.

SOAP

Soap has many uses around the home besides cleaning. Maybe you'll like some of these.

- A bar of soap rubbed on the threads of screws will let the fastener go into hardwoods easier.
- Lubricate a saw blade with a bar of soap.
- That zipper that doesn't glide will zip with ease after you rub the teeth with soap.
- Windows and drawers that are balky will benefit from a soap bar lube job.
- Tiny nail holes in sheetrock are instantly patched by rubbing a bar of soap across the surface.
- Liquid soap or detergent can be used in water to be applied to remove wallpaper. It acts as a wetting agent and helps the water stick to the surface better.
- It also makes for a quick bubble bath!

23
COMING TO GRIPS
The tire chain was invented by Harry D. Weed of Canastota, New York and he got a grip on a patent on this day in 1904. It won't be long before winter when you should think about including a set of chains in the trunk of your car. If all that chain rattling around bugs you, make a holder for each chain from a sleeve made from an old innertube. With the chain unit inside, tie or tape up the ends and you'll have a quieter ride.

24
Cornelius Swarthout got tired of having a short stack of pancakes for breakfast every morning so he invented the waffle iron. He was given a patent for his creation on August 24, 1869.

If you are bothered with a sticking waffle iron, it's probably because the cooking surfaces need to be tempered. This can be done by brushing cooking oil or lard over the irons. Then place slices of bread, also brushed with oil, to cover the entire surface. Close the unit and turn on the heat just long enough to brown the bread. The bread will hold the oil around the waffle grid squares for tempering.

25
After waking up with a stiff back for years, Josiah French sprang into action and invented the bedspring. His efforts were rewarded with the issuance of a patent on this date in 1831.

Lots of older bedsprings creak and groan with just the slightest movement. If your mate is a restless person who tosses and turns all night, and if you're a light sleeper, you may be losing a lot of sleep. You can't oil the springs because it would make too big a mess. However, use a spray wax on all the places where two pieces of metal touch. Now you can rest in peace.

26
FORTY LOVE! Tennis, much as we know it today, was the invention of Major Walter C. Wingfield of Great Britain. He introduced the game on this day in 1873. The game was brought to the United States by Mary Ewing Outerbridge the following year.

After tennis balls have lost their usefulness on the court, they still have some handy uses.

A slit tennis ball makes a good hiding place for jewelry if kept in with the other tennis equipment.

Four slit balls can be used on the feet of a lawn chair so it doesn't scrape the patio or deck.

27

BLACK GOLD

On this day in 1859, Colonel Edwin Laurentine Drake brought in the very first producing oil well. It was drilled in the Oak Creek area of Titusville, Pennsylvania.

Lubricants have taken many other forms and using the right one is often important. Our Lube Guide may help you get off on the right foot.

Lube Guide

The best lube guide is the manufacturer's manual . . . whether it be for an automobile, electric appliance, or what have you. You won't go wrong following their instructions. This guide is just a general home helper to follow when in doubt. Also . . . it's almost as important to not over-lube as it is to under-lube. Regular planned lubrication prevents problems. Seasonal items such as boat motors, lawn mowers, etc., should be lubed as recommended while in use and also when it's time to store them. You can have a complete home lube kit by picking up eight or ten low cost items next time you're in your local hardware store.

USES	LUBRICANT
HINGES	Powdered Graphite—Dripless Machine Oil
LOCKS	Powdered Graphite—Silicone Spray
MOTORS	Small motors should use Household Oil, Medium and Large motors—30 MS Engine Oil
SAW BLADES	Rub with Soap or Paraffin—Silicone Spray
WOODEN DRAWERS	Silicone Spray—Soap—Wax
BELTS (Rubber)	Belt Dressing—Silicone Spray

USES	LUBRICANT
OPEN GEARS	All Purpose Grease if Open-Gear Grease not available
FISHING REELS	Instrument Oil
TRACKS (Sliding Parts)	Dry Moly (Molybdenum Disulfide—Wax—All Purpose Grease
METAL FOR STORAGE	All Purpose Grease—Household Oil—Rust Preventive Paint
FROZEN METAL PARTS (Loosening Bolts)	Penetrating Oil—Iodine—Peroxide
SPROCKETS/CHAINS	All Purpose Grease—Moly-Based Grease
CLOCKS	Instrument Oil
WINDOWS (Home)	Wax for wood—Dry Moly for metal
DRILL BITS	Paraffin—Household Oil
ANYTHING WOOD, PLASTIC, OR RUBBER	Silicone Spray

28

COOL, MAN, COOL

Dr. Schuyler S. Wheeler had just about enough of this August heat so he attached a propeller-like fan blade on a motor shaft and had created the first electric fan. This was back in 1852.

HOUSE-A-TOSIS

Some of those TV ads for room deodorizers really stink . . . but then so do some houses. Often the house odors build up so gradually that we don't notice, but when guests come in, the odor may knock their heads off!

Room deodorizers will mask odors but it's better if you can find and cure the source of the odor.

- Mildew has an offensive odor and is also unsightly. Usually, laundry bleach will do the job on all the fungus you can see. Mildew in a basement may not be seen but still smells. Air out and dry out all damp areas.

- The sink disposer may have bad breath. Clean the insides of the unit to give it kissing sweet breath.

- Cooking odors can become offensive. Use your vent fan when cooking smelly things. Also be sure the filter in the vent fan is clean.

- Not only do you have to take out the garbage regularly, but you should clean and sanitize the receptacle in which the trash is kept.

- Smokers, including a smoking fireplace, add to the household odors and a good airing plus a room deodorizer will help.

Maybe you don't want the place to smell too good, or your guests that used to turn up their noses may move in.

29

KEEPS THE HOT STUFF HOT
AND THE COOL STUFF COOL

Yes, we're talking about the Dewar flask . . . better known today as the thermos bottle. It was conceived by Sir James Dewar of England and introduced on this day in 1892. In addition to keeping food and drink hot or cold, it has a great handyperson use. When you're working where there is no hot water available, carry along a thermos of warm soapy water for cleanup. But remember not to mistake it for a beverage.

30

HOW TO REPLACE CERAMIC TILES

1. Drill a hole in the center of the cracked tile to be removed using a carbide masonry drill bit.
2. If the crack isn't all the way across the surface, score a couple of lines in an "X" with a glass cutter.
3. Now you can use a cold chisel to break and remove the tile without damage to surrounding tiles.
4. Clean away loose material, and chisel the surface to remove lumps.
5. Remove the grout around the opening.
6. There are two ways to restick the new tile. Most were originally set in a masonry mix. We'll tell more about that way after these steps. However, for only one or two tiles, purchase a

can of tile adhesive and apply it to the back of the tile according to directions.

7. Ease the tile into place and press until the tile is even with the surrounding surface.

8. Position the tile so the space for grout is equal all around.

9. Either use tape to hold the tile in place until the adhesive sets or insert toothpick pieces at the bottom and on the sides so it stays.

10. When the adhesive has cured (check the label), fill in the spaces with grout. Buy this in dry form and mix and apply according to the directions on the container. The grout has cement in it, but for just one or two tiles, I use a finger to smooth the grout into place. Then wash away the grout from your hands before the cement has time to harm the skin.

11. After about fifteen minutes, gently remove any grout that got over onto the tiles. If you remove any from the spaces, you'll have to replace it.

12. The next day you can wipe the tiles vigorously to get all traces of the grout off.

13. BE SURE NOT to get water on the grout until it has fully cured according to the label.

If there are many tiles to replace, or if there are big holes in the old cement underneath, use white Portland cement. Butter the tiles with more than enough to fill, and then when you press the tiles in place, the excess will squish out. In most cases, the excess will also fill in the grout joints, and if not, the same mix can be added to fill any spaces.

This same idea is used to reapply a loose tile or soap dish that may have fallen on your foot.

31

NUTS TO YOU

Micah Rugg of Marion, Connecticut invented a machine for trimming the heads of nuts and bolts. This creation put that industry on the road to mass production. He was granted a patent on his machine on this last day of August 1842.

There are many varieties of nuts, bolts, and washers and these two guides will help you know about the more common types.

The Super Handyman Guide to Nuts and Washers

SQUARE
4-sided general
purpose.

FLAT SQUARE NUT
4-sided but smaller.

HEXAGONAL NUT
6-sided general pur-
pose. Heavier duty
than square nut.

**ACORN NUT/
CAP NUT**
Seals threads from
elements. Also for
appearance.

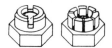

**CAGE NUT/
CLIP NUT**
Slips over edge of
work so nut stays in
place during installa-
tion when nut isn't
visible.

COUPLING NUT
Joins pair of threaded
rods or fasteners.

**NUT/WASHER
COMBO**
Washer is joined to
nut but nut turns free
of washer during
tightening.

KNURLED NUT
Hand tighten with fin-
gers instead of
wrench.

CASTLE NUT
Cotter pin goes
through slots and
hole in bolt to lock in
place.

TEE NUT
Spikes allow nut to be
inserted into wood
where metal threads
are needed.

WING NUT
Hand tightened with
fingers instead of
wrench. Ideal when
something frequently
needs to be removed.

**TOOTHED
WASHER (internal)**
Lock washer that
yields finished look
since teeth are hid-
den by bolt head or
nut.

FLAT WASHER
Protects surface.

**SPRING
LOCK/SPLIT
WASHER**
Most common lock
washer to prevent
loosening by vibra-
tion.

**TOOTHED
WASHER**
(External) Same as
above, except teeth
show.

**COUNTERSUNK
WASHER** Allows use
of countersunk screw
or bolt head without
having to drill coun-
tersink hole. A finish-
ing washer.

The Super Handyman
Machine Screw and Bolt Guide

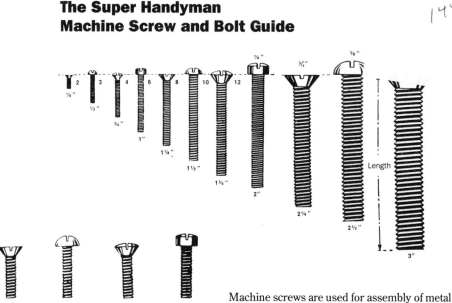

Flat   Round   Oval   Fillister

MACHINE SCREWS. Sizes are designated by length in inches, by diameter in number of the American Screw Gauge for diameters less than ¼ inch, and in fractions of an inch for diameters ¼ inch and larger. Designations are for sizes commonly used.

Machine screws are used for assembly of metal parts and are driven into drilled and tapped holes. Machine screws are most commonly made of mild steel and brass, with four types of head—flat, round, oval, and fillister. They are furnished plain and also with commonly used platings and degrees of finish—nickel, brass, copper, cadmium, electrogalvanized, Parkerized, and zinc-plated.

	Tap Size		
Diameter	Threads per inch	Drill Size no.	Drill Diameter in inches
2	56	51	.0670
3	48	⁵⁄₆₄"	.0781
4	40	43	.0890
6	32	36	.1065
8	32	29	.1360
10	24	25	.1495
12	24	17	.1730
¼"	20	8	.1990
⁵⁄₁₆"	18	F	.2570
³⁄₈"	16	⁵⁄₁₆"	.3125
½"	13	²⁷⁄₆₄"	.4219

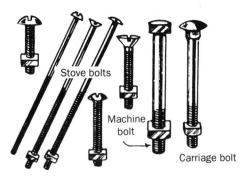

Stove bolts usually are carried in stock in standard sizes with the same types of slotted heads as wood screws. Carriage bolts have a square shoulder under the head that seats firmly into the wood workpiece. Machine bolts have square or hexagonal heads, are installed with a wrench, and are usually used if the parts to be joined are made of metal. Machine and carriage bolts are usually made with full-diameter shanks. Like stove bolts, they are carried in standard sizes in most hardware stores.

SEPTEMBER

- *Don't forget the filter.*
- *Install covers over window air conditioner units.*
- *Properly put your mower away until next season.*
- *Clean and oil other lawn and garden tools for off-season storage.*
- *A pre-season check of the furnace is due.*
- *Take a caulking tour to be sure your home is buttoned up.*
- *Inspect the weatherstripping on all doors and windows.*

1

LOST AND FOUND
The *Titanic,* lost to the depths of the Atlantic Ocean for all these years, was found on this day in 1985.

NOT LOST BUT FOUND ANYWAY
The U.S. space probe, Pioneer 2, transmits evidence of Saturn having two more rings and another moon. The year is 1979.

ALSO FOUND PART II
Eugene McPherson found that he could ride his bike across the entire North American continent in under three weeks and he was the first to do so. The twenty-two-year-old Ohio State student left Santa Monica, California on this day in 1949.

With the start of the school year, you may be picking out a new bike for your school-age youngster. It is very important that the bike be the right size. We parents often think in terms of, "Let's get a size too big . . . the kid will grow into it." It's more important that the bike fit the body NOW!

The seat and the handle bars can be raised as the child grows, but if he starts off with a frame that's too big, he may not have proper control and that could be very dangerous. And before you get a bike with hand brakes, keep in mind that small hands may not be able to properly operate them.

When you get the right bike, make sure the seat and handlebars are properly positioned and securely tightened. Make certain the child knows how to operate everything on the machine and is a competent enough rider to be let out on the streets.

Of course you want lights and reflectors for night and even at dusk. The bike and rider should have high visibility in daylight, too. A colorful bike flag plus bright clothing are good.

With a good properly fitting bike, your child will be getting exercise and training for his own transcontinental bike ride in a few years.

2

THIS DATE IN HISTORY
Today is the birthday of Super Handyman Al Carrell. Why not

celebrate by tackling at least one do-it-yourself project! How about painting that room you've been putting off?

HOW TO PAINT INSIDE

1. Drive in any protruding nail heads and cover them with spackling compound.
2. Patch cracks and holes. (*See how to patch steps on September 6.*)
3. Remove all loose and flaking paint.
4. Clean the walls. (Hopefully that's all you'll have to do.) If there's only a matter of dust, brush or vacuum it away. Any other dirt should be washed off. Airborne grease in a kitchen can be removed with mineral spirits paint thinner. (Caution: It is flammable, so have plenty of ventilation and no flames around.)
5. Remove gloss from all surfaces. The hard way is to sand it away. The easy way is with liquid deglossing chemicals you can buy at the paint store.
6. Remove all furniture, pictures, drapes, and rugs from the room. If you can't move it out, move it out of the way, and cover everything that is there with drop cloths.
7. Mask the trim and anything else you don't want to paint that is adjacent to the area to be coated.
8. Remove the wall plates and remove or loosen light fixtures. Wrap fixtures in plastic.

With the preparation done, you're ready to paint.

1. Mix the paint thoroughly. Pour off about two-thirds of the paint into another bucket. Then stir what's left. Next pour the two back and forth to completely mix.
2. Use the sequence of ceilings first, walls next, and trim last.
3. Paint a border along the edge with a brush. This is called cutting-in.
4. Start with a roller or pad properly filled with paint right next to the cut-in strip.
5. Keep working in strips all the way across the ceiling always working against the wet edge of the previous strip. If you allow a strip to dry before painting against it, you may leave streaks. Be sure to have time to completely finish the ceiling or any wall

without having to stop or start in on a new bucket of paint as there may be a difference in the color.

6. Mix your paint as you go.

7. If you're right-handed, it's best to start in a left-hand corner and work across with up and down strokes from ceiling to floor.

8. Remove all hardware from cabinets and doors to be painted.

9. Use an enamel on the trim.

3

Labor Day was first observed on this day in 1894.

This was also the day on which Jacob Sloat of Sloatsburg, New York converted his cloth mill into a cotton twine factory. The year was 1839 and the factory was soon producing about 6,000 pounds of twine a week.

Did you ever find yourself about to tie a package, but see that you have no knife or razor blade to cut the twine with? Here's a trick to let you snap the string. Follow the drawings and once you get the hang of it, the string will break every time.

For practice purposes, let's assume you need to tie a package for mailing. You have wrapped the string around the package and now you need to break it so you can tie the knot.

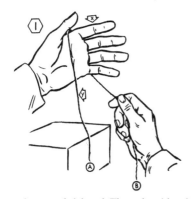

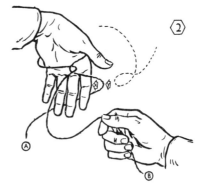

Lay string over left hand. The palm-side of the string will be "A," and the back-side "B." Sec. "A" is coming from the package, and Sec. "B" from ball of twine. Grasp "B" with thumb and forefinger of the right hand and bring it toward you so it is 4 or 5 inches in front of the left hand as shown. Keep points "X" and "Y" in mind for next step. . . .

. . . which is a tricky maneuver with the left hand. The left hand is brought down completely under both Sec. "A" and "B." Point "X" on the left hand loops under point "Y" of the string. Now "A" is to the back of the hand as above. Left hand is now returned to its original position. The tricky maneuver has caused "A" to form a "V" in the palm of the left hand with "B" coming out to right hand from the point at bottom of "V." All this time, the right hand has not moved and is still in front of left hand.

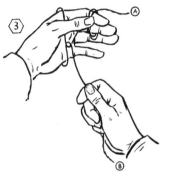

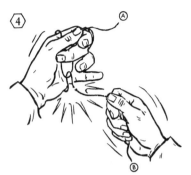

Now twist the fore and middle fingers around Sec. "A" forming loops as above for extra leverage. If the string doesn't look as above, start over.

Gently pull the string tight and adjust the "V" up to the middle or upper part of the palm. Now give a quick outward and downward snap with the right hand. If you have done everything right, the string should break.

An added twist for greater snapping power: before the snap, hold Sec. "B" with right thumb and forefinger, and with the string around the outside of the forefinger, bring it down on the inside of the other three fingers. Close the fingers so the string comes from the inside of the palm at the little finger and then leads to the "V." This gives a better grip and makes the quick snap more effective.

A Super Hint: Start out with a light weight string until you have mastered the technique because if you get the string twisted around wrong, it can really be painful when you give it the snap.

4

GO FOR THE GOLD
In 1972, Mark Spitz won his seventh Olympic gold medal on this day.

This is also the anniversary of the founding of Los Angeles. It was named El Pueblo de Nuestra Señora La Reina de Los Angeles de Porciuncula. L.A. is certainly a lot easier to say.

This day in 1957 is also the date on which the Ford Motor Company started selling the ultimate bomb . . . the Edsel. It was taken off the market in 1959.

WEIGHTS AND MEASURES
Length

12 inches	=	1 foot
3 feet	=	1 yard
5½ yards or 16½ feet	=	1 rod
5280 feet or 1760 yards or 320 rods	=	1 statute mile

6080 feet	=	1 nautical mile
1 knot	=	1 nautical mile per hour
6 feet	=	1 fathom
660 feet	=	1 furlong
7.92 inches	=	1 link
100 links	=	1 chain
80 chains	=	1 statute mile
4 inches	=	1 hand

Area

144 square inches	=	1 square foot
9 square feet	=	1 square yard
160 square rods or 10 square chains	=	1 acre
640 acres	=	1 square mile
A square 207.71003 ft. on each side	=	1 acre or 43,560 sq. ft.

Dry Measure

2 pints	=	1 quart
8 quarts	=	1 peck
4 pecks	=	1 bushel
36 bushels	=	1 chaldron

Liquid Measure

A few grains	=	Less than ⅛ teaspoon
60 drops	=	1 teaspoon
1 teaspoon	=	⅓ teaspoon
1 tablespoon	=	3 teaspoons
2 tablespoons	=	1 fluid ounce
4 tablespoons	=	¼ cup or 2 ounces
5⅓ tablespoons	=	⅓ cup or 2⅔ ounces
8 tablespoons	=	½ cup or 4 ounces
16 tablespoons	=	1 cup or 8 ounces
8 tablespoons	=	1 teacup or 4 ounces
¼ cup	=	4 tablespoons
⅜ cup	=	¼ cup plus 2 tablespoons
⅝ cup	=	½ cup plus 2 tablespoons
⅞ cup	=	¾ cup plus 2 tablespoons
1 cup	=	½ pint or 8 fluid ounces
2 cups	=	1 pint or 16 fluid ounces
1 pint	=	16 fluid ounces
1 quart	=	2 pints or 4 cups or 32 fluid ounces
1 gallon	=	4 quarts

Metric Conversions

1 millimeter	=	.03937 inch
1 centimeter	=	.3937 inch
1 meter	=	39.37 inches or 3.2808 ft. or 1.0936 yards
1 kilometer	=	3280.83 or 1093.61 yards or .62137 mile
1 inch	=	2.54 centimeters
1 foot	=	30.48 centimeters
1 yard	=	.9144 meter
1 mile	=	1.609 kilometers
1 liter	=	1.0567 quarts
1 quart	=	.946 liter
1 gram	=	15.432 grains
1 ounce	=	28.35 grams
1 kilogram	=	2.2046 pounds
1 pound	=	.4536 kilogram

Other

12 dozen	=	1 gross
1 horsepower	=	3,000 foot-pounds per minute
1 cord	=	128 cubic feet, usually piled up 8 ft. x 4 ft. x 4 ft.
1 board foot	=	1 ft. x 1 ft. x 1 inch

5

WHERE THERE'S SMOKE

The use of a smoke screen to conceal the military movement of troops and ships was first demonstrated on this day in 1923. The occasion was a test off Cape Hatteras.

OLD HOUSE TIP

If your older home has a fireplace that hasn't been used and you want to fire it up, check to be sure the chimney wasn't used as an easy way to install electrical wiring, plumbing pipes or anything else. A previous occupant may have intended to never use the fireplace again.

6

HOW TO PATCH

Walls, cracks, and holes are usually patched with spackling paste. It comes in powder form to be mixed or in cans as a ready-to-use compound. For hairline cracks, there are caulk sticks much like fat crayons. All you need do there is rub the stick along the crack. For small cracks and holes:

1. Remove any loose material and cover the area with compound using a putty knife.
2. Be sure the compound is fully dry before painting.

For larger holes, you'll need some backing or the compound will fall down between the walls. Here's one way:

1. Use a knife to remove all loose material.
2. Cut a piece of window screen or hardware cloth a bit larger than the hole.

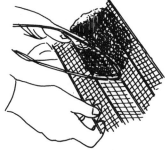

3. Thread a piece of wire through the screen as shown.
4. Push the flexible screen into the hole, holding on to the wire.
5. Pull the wire to bring the backing flat against the inside wall surface.

6. Twist the wire around a pencil to secure the backing in place.

7. Put spackling into the cavity, but don't bring it up to the surface.

8. After it sets, snip the wire and add a second layer to be even with the surface. Use a brush, roller, or putty knife to make the new surface match the rest.

For really large holes, it's best to use a piece of plasterboard and just spackle over the crack around it. Here's a way to keep the patch piece in place:

1. Cut out an area around the hole that is a rectangular shape for easier patch matching.

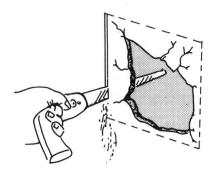

2. Select a scrap board about six inches longer than the widest span of the hole.

3. To secure this backing piece on the inside of the hollow wall, either put screws through the wall to secure each end of the board, or put spackling on each end and hold it in place until it's secure.

4. When the backing board is secure, butter all four edges of the patch plus the center part that will touch the board, and slip it into the opening. Hold it there until the spackling starts to set up.

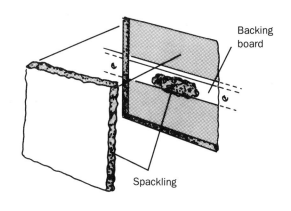

Backing board

Spackling

5. After the patch has set up, texture over it to match the rest of the wall. (Texturing compound is available in small quantities, and it can be brushed or rolled on. The texturing can be matched using a roller or brush, and the compound is slow enough in setting to give you time to play around. I'd experiment with texturing on a scrap board if it's new to you.)

7

WHERE THE ROAD MEETS THE RUBBER

A synthetic rubber patch for asphalt roads was used on this day in 1948 on a stretch of blacktop road in Akron, Ohio.

Blacktop drives in the home are easily repaired when potholes develop. No longer do you need to have a heater that melts the foul-smelling-tarlike patching compound. There are cold-patch compounds that you buy in a sack and then just pour into the hole. The material is tamped down and more added to bring the patch up to the level of the surrounding surface.

Even though it's called cold-patch, it works better on a warm sunny day.

After five days, apply a sealer over the surface. It's just that simple!

8

BEAM ME UP SCOTTY!

On this date in 1966, the series *Star Trek* made its debut as it was beamed into American homes via TV.

The beam from a flashlight must be directed to the work or it's no good. When you're working under the car, it's difficult to steady the beam so it hits the work since you probably need both hands for things other than holding the flashlight. A soup can can help. With the flashlight in the can, it will be held at an angle but upright. It's easy to move the can around so the light beams up exactly where it's needed.

9

ROCK AND ROLL

The Lumberman's Association of America held the very first Log Rolling Championship on Lumberman's Day, September 9, 1898. It's written in the log that the winner was Tommy Fleming of Eau Claire, Wisconsin.

The nearest most of us get to a log is in connection with those logs we use for the fireplace. If you end up with logs so big that the only way to move them is to roll them, they're probably too big. But a child's sled may make carrying big or normal sized logs a lot easier. The little red wagon can also help.

Or, how about cutting a foot long section from an old car tire and poking holes in it to add rope handles. The logs ride inside the tire.

10

The first coast-to-coast paved highway went from New York City to San Francisco. The opening of the Lincoln Highway was proclaimed on this day in 1913.

It was not recorded when the first pothole appeared in the 3,300 mile long stretch. However, holes do occur in concrete. Look at your own walks and drives. The key to patching such holes so they will last is to use a bonding adhesive. This is a milky chemical that makes the old and the new stick together. Without it, the patch has been known to come loose before the mix has fully cured.

Buy this bonding agent where you buy cement and then follow the directions for proper use.

11

The patent on the collapsible tube was awarded to John Rand on this date in 1841. These early tubes were made of lead but many tubes are now made of plastic. Glue, toothpaste, ointment, paints, caulking, and dozens of other products are sold in tubes. Sometimes the contents get onto the threads and the cap becomes sealed in place.

This is particularly bad in the case of glues and caulks. It never has to happen if you'll coat the threads with petroleum jelly when the tube is first opened.

12

English explorer Henry Hudson sailed into New York via the river that now bears his name on this day in 1609. Often today's pollution in this and other rivers might make it easier to *walk* on the water than steer a boat through the muck and mire.

This day is also important to all who write and draw because on this day in 1795, a Frenchman, Nicolas Jacques Conte, announced a new pencil-making process. He mixed clay with graphite to form a hardened "lead." Actually, there is no lead in a lead pencil.

Since graphite is also a good lubricant, you can use a soft lead pencil to help lubricate inside a lock. Rub the key back and forth over the pencil tip. When inserted in the lock and worked back and forth, the lubricant is distributed.

13

Henry H. Bliss became the first automobile fatality on this day in 1899. While getting off of a streetcar in New York City, he was hit by a car driven by Arthur Smith.

Unfortunately, these days thousands of lives are lost to auto accidents each year. Here is a quickie checklist to make your car safer.

- Be sure the windshield wipers work and that the blades are in good condition.
- All rearview mirrors must be inspected.
- Defrosters can aid your visibility during winter driving, only if the system works properly.
- All lights, including headlights, tail lights, brake and turn indicator lights should be checked regularly.
- Inspect tires regularly and be sure they have proper pressure.
- Brake and steering problems usually show signs of trouble before they become unsafe. Take action to repair at the first signs.

- Carbon monoxide kills even without an accident. Be sure the exhaust system is okay.

- Make sure the horn works.

- As winter approaches, put a bag of kitty litter in the trunk. Sprinkle the litter under your "power" tires (depending on whether you have front- or rear-wheel drive) for extra traction on ice if needed.

- Your seat belts won't prevent your having a wreck but if you do, they can save your life . . . so be sure there are no flaws in the belts.

14

QUIET PLEASE

The first sound absorbing material to receive a U.S. patent did so on this day in 1915. It was the invention of Carl Gebhard Muench of Saint Paul.

If you live in a noisy neighborhood, Mother Nature can help in blocking out some of the din. Hedges and other plants block and absorb some of the traffic, dog barking, and siren wailing sounds. Trees can also help. However, this is for the long haul as plants have to grow to do any good. A fence or wall goes to work on sound control as soon as it's erected. The taller and more solid the fence or wall, the better.

So while you're improving the looks of your great outdoors, you're probably also making a kinder and gentler world inside.

15

HI HO SILVER

On this date in 1949, the Lone Ranger made his debut on TV. Almost every program ended with some of the townfolk asking, "Who was that masked man?"

16

Possibly man's greatest achievement occurred on this day in 1955 with the introduction of Play-Dough.

This day in 1782 also marked the first official use of the Great Seal of the United States. The seal was placed on a document giving

General George Washington the authority to negotiate an exchange of prisoners of war with the British.

There is also a "great seal" you can use. All exterior surfaces around the house are subjected to moisture and those materials that are porous can often greatly benefit by having a coat of sealer applied. Otherwise, your home can suffer thousands of dollars worth of damage from water.

Here are some likely candidates for sealing.

All concrete work such as drives, walks, pool decking, and patios should be sealed. Brick may also be in need of such a treatment and don't forget the brick chimney.

Exterior wood that isn't painted should be sealed. This even includes decks that are made from pressure-treated lumber. Don't forget wood shingles, window boxes, shutters, or wooden windows and doors, including the garage door.

Canvas awnings will probably last longer if protected by a sealer.

17

SNAP BACK! On this date in 1820, the rubber band was created by Thomas Hancock of London. He first marketed it as a way to have elastic tops to waistbands of clothing. The rubber band, as we know it today, has hundreds of home uses.

- A rubber band around the paint can will hold a paint rag handy.

- When gluing, a rubber band may be stretched around the object to provide clamping pressure.

- A wide rubber band around the end of the top step of a step ladder will hold small tools.

- Wrap several rubber bands around the handle of a screwdriver to prevent it from rolling away. The same idea works on a flashlight.

- Use a rubber band to hold a pen light to the top of your drill.

MAKE YOUR OWN

Old auto and bike innertubes can be cut to make lots of heavy-duty rubber bands. Worn out rubber gloves will also yield a bonanza of rubber bands of many different sizes.

18

The first power-driven lumber mill in what is now the United States was in Maine, the Pine Tree State. The saw was powered by water. It was established on this day in 1641 in the community of Georgeanna, which is now York.

Did you ever wonder why they call it a 2x4? "Of course," you say, "It's because the board is 2 inches thick and 4 inches wide."

Wrong, pine-knot breath. That's the nominal size, but after the wood is seasoned and planed, it measures only 1½ inches x 3½ inches.

Here are the nominal and actual sizes for the lumber we use.

Nominal (in inches)	Actual
1x3	¾ x 2½
1x4	¾ x ½
1x6	¾ x 5½
1x8	¾ x 7¼
1x10	¾ x 9¼
1x12	¾ x 11¼
2x3	1½ x 2½
2x4	1½ x 3½
2x6	1½ x 5½
2x8	12½ x 7¼
2x10	1½ x 9¼
2x12	1½ x 11¼

You'll be happy to know that an eight-foot long 2x4 will actually be eight feet long.

19

A CLEAN SWEEP

The first carpet sweeper that was practical for home use was invented by Melville Rueben Bissell of Grand Rapids, Michigan. He was granted a patent on the device on this day in 1878. The sweeper was hand-powered and as the unit was rolled back and forth, it rotated brushes to sweep the floor. The invention was the forerunner to today's improved version that still bears the name Bissell.

Regular care means better looking and longer lasting carpets and rugs. Dirt and grit can act much like sandpaper to cause an abrasive action that will cut fibers and accelerate wear. Surface dirt, dust, and airborne grease can cause discoloration. Regular care can remove these problems.

The sweeper should be used on a daily basis to remove dirt and grit before it is ground in deep. Just a few passes will remove dust, dirt, and pet hair.

You should vacuum at least once a week. This removes surface dirt as well as embedded grit.

Get on spills immediately and they probably won't become stains.

Finally, shampoo at least a couple of times each year. This removes greasy dirt.

20

SOMETHING'S COOKING! George B. Simpson of Washington, D.C. invented the electric range and was given a patent on this day in 1889.

Most electric ranges have four burners of two different sizes. If one burner no longer heats, remove it and replace it with the other of the same size. If that one heats, you know the fault is in the burner. If it does not, the problem is either in the wiring to that burner or in the control for the burner.

21

IT'S A GAS! On this day in 1875, Thaddeus Lowe was awarded a patent on the improvement in processing gas for heating purposes. Gas is a popular and economical fuel for home use.

If you ever smell a heavy gas odor, **take it seriously.** Immediately turn off any flames, open doors and windows, and get the family out of the house. Do not flip any light switches, use anything electrical, or even use the phone. The slightest spark could ignite the gas. Turn off the main gas shutoff valve if it's located outside the house. Use a neighbor's phone to call the gas utility company to report the problem.

22

YOU LIGHT UP MY LIFE

Today is Debbie Boone's birthday. She was born in Hackensack, New Jersey on September 22, 1956. While she continues to perform as a singer, she has yet to come close to her big hit single, "You Light Up My Life."

Lighting is an important consideration in your life at home or in the shop. The colors used on your walls, ceilings, and floors can have a tremendous effect on how available light is utilized because each color has a different value. The chart below gives you the approximate percentages for matte finish surfaces. A glossy finish in the same color would result in slightly higher reflection.

REFLECTION PERCENTAGES*					
White	82%	Powder Blue	63%	Coffee	28%
Ivory	78%	Aqua	61%	Kelly Green	25%
Yellow	75%	Apricot	59%	Red	21%
Peach	71%	Gold	54%	Chalk Board Green	20%
Light Pink	70%	Rose	46%	Brown	15%
Beige	69%	Medium Gray	45%	Walnut Paneling	10%
Light Gray	65%	Orange	35%	Dark Royal Blue	8%
Lemon Yellow	64%				

* Values vary slightly with different paint manufacturers.

23

THE DOG DAYS? This is the anniversary of then vice presidential candidate Richard M. Nixon's famous "Checkers Speech." On national TV, Nixon was responding to allegations that a private fund had been set up for his expenses. He denied any wrongdoing and said he would return any gifts except Checkers, the family dog. The cocker spaniel had been a gift to his daughters. The picture of the dog on the TV screen had the desired effect and the Eisenhower/Nixon ticket rolled on to victory.

If you walk your dog daily, cold weather can have an effect on the pads of his feet. After each trek, clean Fido's paws and rub petroleum jelly on and around the pads.

24

The Brooklyn Dodgers played their last game at Ebbets Field on this day in 1957. The franchise was then moved to Los Angeles.

This was also the day in 1874 on which Robert W. Johnson and George J. Seabury came up with a medicated adhesive plaster that would later be called the Band-Aid. Johnson later set up Johnson & Johnson, now a giant corporation still making Band-Aids. We don't know what happened to Seabury.

We do know that band-aids are useful in other ways around the house. Like as a pad for clamps and pliers to keep the tool from biting into the work.

25

Baltimore resident Thomas Moore got tired of spoiled food and so he invented the first refrigerator . . . which was really just an ice box. It consisted of an inner box surrounded by insulation and then encased in an outer box. By putting ice in with the food, the food stayed fresh much longer. On this date in 1803, he issued a booklet describing the new ice box, which he called the refrigerator.

The same principle that Thomas Moore came up with can save all your frozen foods if you should ever have a power failure or if the refrigerator should conk out. Just keep a supply of dry ice in the freezer compartment, enough to keep the temperature between 0°F and 5°F. A smaller amount of dry ice can keep the temperature in the refrigerator part at a safe level of 35°F.

26

The first American cement was invented by David Saylor and he received a patent for his process on this day in 1871.

Cement is the "glue" that holds the concrete together when sand, gravel, and water are mixed in proper proportions. In mixing, it is very important that every rock and every grain of sand be coated with the cement.

In figuring out how much concrete is needed for a project, you should figure the volume in either cubic feet or for bigger jobs, in cubic yards. A cubic yard is 27 cubic feet. The formula to find cubic feet is: width (feet) x length (feet) x thickness (inches) divided by 12 = cubic feet. Use the same width x length x thickness but divide it by 324 and you'll get the number of cubic yards.

27 CLOSE COVER BEFORE STRIKING

Back on this date in 1892, a man named Joshua Pusey got a patent on book matches. The small striker area on a match book cover is a good little abrasive strip for putting a quick edge on a pocket knife or a point on a pencil.

But this day in the history of abrasives is more important because of Norton Company of Worcester, Massachusetts. It was the day they released a paper that was read before the Electrochemical Society of New York. It told of a new abrasive that could be used commercially to perform work that previously could only be done with diamond dust.

MOST WIDELY USED COATED ABRASIVES			
ABRASIVE	BACKING	GRADES (readily available)	BROAD USES
FLINT	Paper (A, C, & D weights)	Extra coarse through extra fine	Small hand sanding wood-removing paint. Clogs fast but very cheap. Great for gummy surfaces that would clog any paper used.
GARNET	Paper (A, C, & D weights)	Very coarse through very fine	Hand shaping and sanding of wood. Also for cork and composition board. Cuts better and lasts longer than flint.
ALUMINUM OXIDE	Paper (A, C, & D weights)	Very coarse through very fine	Hand or power sanding or shaping of wood. Also for metals, paint smoothing, or end-grain sanding.
	Cloth (X)	Very coarse through fine	Mostly used for belt sanders.
SILICON CARBIDE	Waterproof paper (A weight)	Very coarse through super fine	To smooth coats on wood, metal, etc. For sanding floors, glass, or plastics. Used wet with water or oil.
EMORY	Cloth (X & J weights)	Very coarse through fine	General light metal polishing. Removing rust and corrosion from metal. Can be used wet or dry.
CROCUS	Cloth (J weight)	Very fine only	Super high-gloss finishing for metals.

28

Lots of our headaches were solved on this day in 1853, although we didn't know it at the time. This was the day when an Alsatian chemist named Charles Gerhardt came up with acetylsalicylic acid which we now know as aspirin. It wasn't recognized, however, as a pain reliever until the Bayer folks got hold of it in 1899.

The little metal tins that aspirin come in have been good for solving small home headaches. The tins will hold several razor blades so they can be carried in the tool box or pocket without getting ruined or cutting your fingers. Small tacks, brads, and nails can be carried in your pocket in one of these small containers without your getting stabbed.

29

AT THE SOUND OF THE TONE
The first telephone answering machine was created on this day in 1950.

Ditto for the first eraser, created by English chemist Joseph Priestley in the year 1770. He is the Englishman who discovered that rubber could be used to remove pencil marks by rubbing . . . hence the name "rubber."

The eraser has some other uses around the home. You can often erase light rust away. The typewriter eraser works better than a pencil eraser. However, the pencil type will often reach back into places where your hand can't get to.

Try using an eraser to remove spots on wallpaper. Don't rub hard enough to erase the pattern on the paper.

30

LET THERE BE LIGHT
And there was. It happened on this day in 1882 when the first hydroelectric power plant was opened in Appleton, Wisconsin.

It was not UL-approved but your next plug replacement for a large appliance or tool will be up to snuff if you'll use the Underwriter's Knot.

The underwriters' knot is a special method of attaching a cord to a plug so that the wires will not be pulled out of the plug if suddenly subjected to a yank. It's quite simple to do . . . just follow the sketches.

1

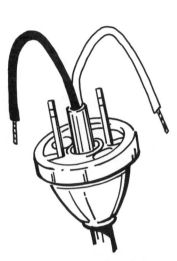

Pull out about 3 inches of wire.

2

3

4

Pull the knot tight and then pull the cord down into the plug. In most cases it will fit down into the space in the plug. Twist the bare wire so there are no loose strands.

5

Bring each wire around a prong. Hook wire around screw in same direction as screw turns. Tighten down and it should look like this . . . when looking down on the knot and plug. You will note it forms a sort of "S" if properly tied . . . this "S" stands for super.

OCTOBER

- *Did I mention filters?*
- *Install storm windows.*
- *Lay in your supply of firewood. Bring some inside in case of bad weather.*
- *Reexamine the fireplace for cracked mortar joints and inspect the chimney for any blockage.*
- *Protect outside hydrants from the cold.*
- *Check to be sure the car has radiator coolant.*
- *Take a caulking tour before it's too cold to do so.*

1

LESS MESS

The first litter law in the country was passed by the state of Oregon. It went into effect on this date in 1972. The bill outlawed pull-tab cans and nonreturnable bottles. Since then, hundreds of anti-litter laws have been passed and yet we still have a terrible litter problem.

The more ways we can find to use things that would ordinarily be thrown away, the fewer the number of these items that will end up as litter. So, let's get off our cans and start to think. Here are some thought-provoking uses for all sorts of metal cans.

The cans have already proven themselves as containers. Remove the lids and let them continue to hold all sorts of other things. Decorate a beverage or soup can to hold pencils. Use cans with plastic lids to hold powdered compounds in the garage or shop. Mount various sized cans on the wall with the open side facing out and you have all the pigeonholes you could ever need.

Form a hose hanger with pigeonholes by clustering a bunch of cans and mounting them on the wall to form a sort of circle.

Make a sleeve from several coffee cans with both ends cut from all but the bottom can. Stack them one atop the other and tape them together. You can store dowels, metal rods, small molding strips and other long items.

Put six cans without lids back in the plastic looped holder and you have a six-pack tote for several small items.

Since the average person in the United States uses about 400 cans a year, you should find a use for 400 cans for each person in your family. Hope these ideas get you started.

2

UNCANNY!

J. Osterhoudt was probably always losing his can opener because he invented the first can with its own key for opening. He was granted a patent on this creation on this day in 1866. There are still some cans that come with these keys and if you get one, attach it to your key ring and you'll always have a pocket screwdriver.

3

VIDEO HISTORY

The first videotape recording on magnetic tape was made on this date in 1952 at Bing Crosby Enterprises.

If you have a home video camera, use it to make a record of all your belongings. As you shoot the footage of each item or group, narrate on tape to describe what is being shown. Include size, price, brand name, model, serial numbers, and anything else that would help to identify the item.

Of course, you'll want to tape all of the valuables such as jewelry, furs, art, and silver, but also shoot *all* the belongings in your home—including clothing. Don't forget the tools and materials in the shop and garage.

When you have all the stuff on tape keep the cassette in your safety deposit box. If there is ever a fire or burglary, you'll have less trouble with the insurance company and in the case of theft, the police will be better equipped to identify your belongings.

4

THE KEY TO SECURITY

Joseph Bramah of Yorkshire, England traveled to London on this date in 1784 and challenged any and everyone to pick open his new invention, a padlock. Nobody could do it so he started a thriving business.

Most burglars couldn't pick their way out of a pay toilet . . . but they don't have to. In too many cases, we leave doors or windows unlocked. If we do lock them, the locks are often poorly made, and a simple prybar allows the crook to open your home quicker than you could with the key.

Many entry locks are spring catch locks and a credit card can be pushed into the crack between the door and frame to retract the spring catch and the thief is inside.

All exterior doors should have sturdy deadbolt locks. Many times, the new lock will fit in the same holes as the old. If not, there are auxiliary deadbolts that can be installed above the old lockset. Now you have two locks.

INSTALLING A DEADBOLT

It's easy to install such a lock. There will be a paper template that fits around the door's edge so you know exactly where to drill. It will also indicate the size hole. A hole saw in a power drill is the best way to drill the hole for the lockset.

Use a proper size bit for the hole in the edge of the door for the bolt. Then mortise out for the bolt plate. You will also mortise for the striker plate in the door frame.

In the installation of the lockset, remember that the screws that hold the front part and back part must be inside the house.

If you make it harder for the burglar to get in, he'll probably go on until he finds easier (non) pickings.

5

Paper has been around for centuries and may have been reinvented in different parts of the world. The first record of paper, however, goes back to China in the year 105. Prior to that time, there had been papyrus. This was replaced by parchment. Ts'i Lun, the minister of public works under Emperor Ho-Ti, was interested in something better to write and draw on and discovered a way to make paper.

Thousands of items are now made from paper. One of the handier examples is the paper towel, which can be used in many different ways.

You should install a rack for paper towels in the shop and garage and also keep a roll in the trunk of your car. Of course, paper towels blot up all sorts of spills. A damp paper towel will also blot up tiny slivers of glass from a broken mirror.

If you run out of coffee filters, use a paper towel instead. A similar use is when your tea bag breaks. Pour the tea through a paper towel and it strains out all particles.

For shop use, maybe you don't need a full-sized paper towel. Use an electric carving knife to cut the roll in half and double your pleasure.

6

HAPPY BIRTHDAY

It's the anniversary of the birth of George Westinghouse, the man who invented the air brake for trains, an improved gas meter, and hundreds of other things. He also introduced the idea of alternating current in electricity. He founded over fifty companies including Westinghouse Electric Company. He was born on October 6, 1846.

Alternating current (AC) was violently opposed by Thomas A. Edison, who had developed a system for providing electricity to homes using direct current (DC). His DC system worked fine as long as the home was within a couple of miles of the power plant. Otherwise, the homeowner would have to have a generator on site. With Westinghouse's AC, electrical service could be sent along wires for hundreds of miles.

Thanks to Westinghouse, electricity is available throughout the country.

7

WHERE AM I?

Without the magnetic compass, a lot of folks would be lost half the time. The first compass was fairly crude. It consisted of a needlelike pointer made of magnetic iron which was placed atop a piece of cork and set afloat on a container of water. The point was attracted to the north pole and would point in that direction. The compass took a big step forward when a Mediterranean navigator named Dominick de Vasco created the 32-point compass. He is said to have introduced this new gadget on a voyage that departed from Italy on this date in 1384.

The same principle is used in the magnetic stud finder. This is a device that locates studs behind a sheet rock wall. A regular old Boy Scout compass will also help in this search. The arrow will be diverted by the nails used to attach the sheetrock to the studs. When you locate the nails, you know where the studs are.

8

FIRE DAY! This is a big day for fires because the first recorded forest fire of any consequence in this country occurred on this date in 1871. It happened in Wisconsin just north of Green Bay and destroyed over a million and a quarter acres of timberland.

Today also marks the anniversary of the Great Chicago Fire which also happened on this day in 1871. The blame was placed on Mrs. O'Leary's cow. Supposedly, the cow kicked over a lantern in the barn and a large part of the toddling town was burned down.

Every day in America, there are almost 2300 house fires plus almost a thousand other structures that burn. Hopefully, this will never happen to you, but if it does, here are some things to do after the fire has been put out.

CLEANING UP AFTER A FIRE

First, there are firms that specialize in fire and water damage restoration. These outfits do everything from cleaning up to helping with your insurance claim. They take care of getting rid of the water, deodorizing, and removal of carpets and rugs. The good ones will start to work as soon as the firemen allow them to enter.

If you'll be doing it yourself, here are some things to remember:

- Before using electricity in the house, make sure it is safe to do so. The fire may have damaged wiring. Water may have made it unsafe to use electricity.

- Contact the insurance company or companies that will be involved so that they can get an adjuster on the scene.

- As soon as you can, photograph or videotape everything that was damaged by the fire. This will help in your dealings with the insurance companies.

- If entry doors and windows are no longer secure, board up the openings.

- You may have to move valuables to another location for safekeeping.

- Move wet carpets, rugs, and padding outside for drying.

- Ventilate to help dry the house, but also rent fans, blowers, and dehumidifiers to speed up the process.

- Use a vacuum cleaner to remove soot and ashes from all horizontal surfaces. Vacuum all upholstered pieces.

- Clothing and drapes will probably have to be dry cleaned, but make sure the dry cleaner is equipped to handle the removal of smoke odor.

- Get rid of all foodstuffs that have been subjected to high heat. Ask a pharmacist about medicines that might have been affected.

Be thankful that you're still around to worry about all this damage.

9

MONEY TALK

On this day in 1792, the mint in Philadelphia coined the first silver half-dimes.

Which brings to mind a great homemade silver polish formula. You'll need:

> 1 cup soap flakes
> 1 cup whiting
> 1 tablespoon ammonia
> 2 cups boiling water

Mix the soap flakes, whiting, and ammonia in a pan and add the boiling water. Stir until all solids are gone. When the mix is cool, store it in a tightly sealed glass jar. To use, apply with a soft cloth and rub to shine. Rinse and wipe dry. Better wear your sunglasses!

10

RACK 'EM UP

Phelan and Collender of New York offered a $10,000 prize to the best substitute for an ivory billiard ball. John Wesley Hyatt was the winner and received a patent for his invention on October 10, 1865— as well as the ten grand.

To keep the cue ball white and also to clean real ivory piano keys, make a paste of hydrogen peroxide and whiting. Smear this on and leave it for an hour. Then wipe off the dried paste with a sponge dampened with hydrogen peroxide.

11

Even before there was an energy crisis, somebody was thinking insulation. John Thomas and James Slayter obtained a patent on this day in 1938 for a process of making glass wool. We now know it as fiberglass, the popular insulating material.

If you have a crawl space under floors and notice that you have cold feet in the winter, it's an easy thing to do to add insulating batts between the floor joists under the floor.

A popular way to hold the batts in place is with chicken wire. Staple strips of chicken wire at right angles to the floor joists, leaving ample room to slide the insulation in place.

Remember that the facing on the batts goes up toward the living area. Don't worry about any space between the batts and the floor as the dead air pocket also has insulating qualities.

12

OLD HOUSE TIP

While there are many sources of reproductions of old-style plumbing fixtures, locksets, and other materials for the old house, you can sometimes find the real thing. Wrecking companies often salvage everything in an old building and sell the stuff. Sometimes you can find old brick, bathtubs, tiles, and other things that are not being made any longer. These may give your restoration a more authentic look.

13

SAFE AT HOME

The first motion detector security alarm was invented by Samuel Bagno of New York City. He obtained a patent for his gadget on this day in 1953. Motion detector lights are a great addition to the outside of your home. They light up when anybody comes into range. These should not be the extent of your security system, but they do discourage prowlers.

14

A landmark arbitration case between the United States and Mexico was heard and the decision and award announced on October 14, 1902. Many homeowner problems are now being solved through arbitration. It's much nicer and less costly than going to court. If you have a dispute with a contractor or tradesman, why not look into arbitration. Most major cities will have several arbitration service companies.

15

This is actually National Grouch Day. Be nice to some old coot because grouches need tender loving care, too.

On October 15, 1881, the first fishing magazine in the United States was spawned. It was published in Philadelphia and was named the *American Angler.* One of the "joys" of fishing is cleaning your catch. Here's a trick to use when scaling a fish. Place the fish on a board or log and spear its tail with an icepick. This will anchor it as you scale toward the head.

With this chore made easier, maybe you'll be a little less grouchy.

16

LIGHTEN UP

The light bulb made a leap forward on this day in 1928 when Marvin Pipkin got his patent on his process of frosting the inside of the bulb. Previously, the bulbs were frosted on the outside. The new way meant a longer lasting bulb with less absorption of light. This new bulb also collected less dust.

Some say that long-life bulbs are also a leap forward. You've seen the ads saying "they last three times as long!" They may cost a little bit more, but not three times as much as regular bulbs.

But do they work? Well, yes they do last longer. They do because the filament operates at a lower temperature. But in doing this, they give off less light while using the same amount of electricity as the regular bulb. To get the same amount of light as with a regular bulb, you'd have to go for a larger wattage which would then consume more electricity.

For the best illumination for the buck, regular bulbs have a little edge. But where the amount of light isn't critical, long-life bulbs can make sense.

17

IT'S A GAS! The first gas meter used in the United States was patented on this date in the year 1834. It was the invention of James Bogardus and was called the "gasometer."

The cut-off for most gas meters is similar to the one shown. The hole in the handle enables the utility company to lock the meter if you don't pay your bills. Since that's not a problem (right?), use the

171

hole to run a string through. Then tie on an inexpensive wrench of the right size to be on hand for a quick shut off in an emergency.

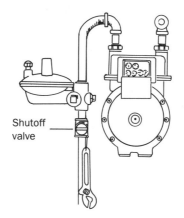

Shutoff valve

18 Charles Mason turned to his partner Jerry Dixon and said, "We gotta draw the line somewhere." And so they did. The Mason-Dixon line was established in 1767.

HAVE A BLAST
This also marks the date in 1870 on which Benjamin Tilghman received a patent on his process called sandblasting.

Sometimes people hire sandblasters to clean brick or stone walls on their homes. It certainly can work, but the down side is that sand can enter your home through even the smallest of cracks. Also, the sand may remove some of the surface of the brick or stone, leaving you with a pitted facing.

Before you decide on sand, look into the other methods which include blasting by water, steam, or chemicals. There are many different chemicals and your selection would depend on the type of dirt and material involved.

19 ### HAVE A BLAST PART II
The first blast furnace using coal was the Pioneer, put into action in Pottsville, Pennsylvania by Benjamin Perry on October 19, 1839. It could turn out twenty-eight tons of foundry iron per week.

That's a lot of potential rust. If you have iron pieces that you're going to store, why not use drained crankcase oil from the car to protect them. Just brush the oil on. It's a way to use something that too often ends up as a problem to get rid of.

20

FEATHERED FRIENDS

The United States and Great Britain agreed on the first international migratory bird legislation and it was ratified by the Brits on this day in 1916.

Here's a bird feeding idea you might like. Take several pine cones and tie strings around them at the top. Melt and blend a half cup each of bacon drippings and peanut butter. Roll each cone in this mix and as it starts to solidify, roll again in birdseed. Hang these in your trees and be prepared for a big bird migration to your yard.

21

You can probably tell that October is a big month in lighting. The very first incandescent electric light bulb was invented on this day in 1879. This was the original created by Thomas Edison.

If you'd like a one-of-a-kind light fixture that would make old Tom proud, it's easy. Get a number of those double sockets that are designed to screw into a single socket to make room for two bulbs. Start with the hanging single socket and by putting the double sockets together, they start to branch out all over the place.

When you get the shape you think you'll like, install 7 1/2 watt bulbs in all the empty sockets. With the fixture lit up, you can add or subtract sockets or bulbs to get it just the way you wish.

22

HOW TO FIX DOORS

For the hard-to-close door:
1. Tighten the hinge screws. Even slight looseness can let the door sag enough to bind. If a screw won't tighten down, the hole has become enlarged. Pack the hole with toothpicks, break them off flush, and reinsert the screw.
2. If there are no loose screws, but there is a gap on the hinge side between door and frame, insert a shim between the hinge and the frame. To do this, loosen the screws and cut a piece of shirtboard to fit. Make slits so the shim can slip past the screws. Retighten screws. If the door binds only at the top or bottom of

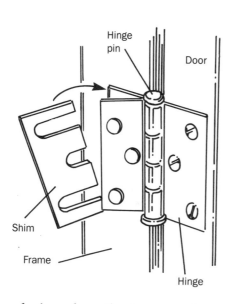

the latch side edge, you may need to shim out the hinge at the opposite end of the door from the binding to counteract the problem. Let a wedge hold the door up while hinge screws are loosened.

3. If the door is swollen, you may have to plane some off the door. If it sticks along the top, use a plane, sandpaper, rasp, or surform tool to remove the desired amount. This can be done with the door still in place. For planing edges, the door must be removed.

4. When a door won't open or close because the house has settled, sometimes you can use a mallet and a padded block to tap against the frame to correct the problem.

For a door that won't latch:

1. Look at the position of the bolt and the strike plate with the door closed to ascertain why they are not engaging.

2. If the bolt is too high or too low to fit into the opening, often you can file a tiny bit off the bolt to make connections. Sometimes you can remove the plate from the jamb and file it off too. If

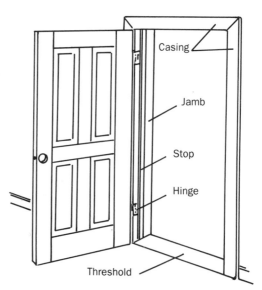

there's too much difference, reposition the striker plate by cutting out additional mortise to allow for its being moved up or down.
3. If the bolt doesn't come out far enough, see if the mechanism is stuck, and clean and lubricate. If that's not the case, try shimmying either the striker plate to move it toward the door, or the hinges to move the door toward the plate.

23

IT'S A RINGER! The first National Horseshoe Pitching Tournament was held in Kellerton, Iowa and it was held on this day in 1915. Frank Jackson was the winner. As most of us know, the horseshoe is a symbol of good luck. But you must hang the horseshoe with the open end facing up . . . or all the luck will fall out.

It's not so lucky, however, if your kids try to pitch horseshoes inside the house. Make a less lethal set from an old auto tire. Slice through the tire to make one-inch-thick slabs. The shape of the tire yields some horseshoe look-alikes that will do much less damage.

24

WAKE UP! The first United States patent for an alarm clock was issued on this day in 1876 to Seth Thomas of Thomaston, Connecticut. (There's no truth to the rumor that he would have gotten the patent a day earlier but he overslept.)

If you have trouble hearing or responding to the alarm clock in the morning, put your TV and the bedroom lights on a timer that is set to turn everything on when it's time to arise. You'll be blasted out of bed!

25

The very first U.S. trademark to be registered, Numero Uno, was by the Averill Chemical Paint Company of New York City.

Name-brand paint is usually a safer bet than paint from somebody you've never heard of. Granted, there are some name-brand paints that aren't top quality. The good paint dealer will be able to tell you which are his best lines. Go for the top of the line. Painting isn't all that much fun so you want it to last as long as possible.

26

Hamilton Erastus Smith got tired of his wife having to bend over a scrub board to wash his clothes and so he invented the first washing machine. It employed a hand crank so his wife still had to do hard labor. But if you run across one of those old wash boards, it's a nice collector's item. It also makes a dandy surface for working the paint out of brushes as you clean them. That rippled surface helps a lot.

27

DO YOU HAVE THE TIME? Although the wristwatch was invented back in 1790, it was strictly for women. It was not until 1880 that an order from the German Admiralty ordered that artillery officers wear a wristwatch. That order issued on October 27, 1880 started a trend in other branches of the military and in other countries.

The outdoorsman can find his way even without a compass if he has his wristwatch. Point the hour hand toward the sun and south will lie in the middle of the angle formed by the hour hand and the numeral 12. North will be directly opposite. This doesn't help all that much at night.

28

The Public Works Administration created the Emergency Housing Corporation. This corporation was authorized on this date in 1933. This led to the creation of Federal Housing Authority. So we have the PWA, the EHC, and FHA.

We don't need the government to tell us about emergency housing. It happens every time the in-laws come to visit. What do we do with all these extra people? How about adding extra space to the house? Instead of going up or out, why not convert? The attic, basement, or garage offer excellent opportunities to convert one less functional type of space into living space.

Since the structural part of the new room has already been done, this looks like a possible do-it-yourself project. You're only faced with covering walls, ceilings, and floors with a basement or garage conversion. The attic requires only minor framing before its requirements are the same.

With the extra living space, the emergency housing problem is suddenly only a pest control problem.

29

BLACK TUESDAY! October 29, 1929 was the day the New York Stock Market crashed. Only four days earlier, President Herbert Hoover had said, "The fundamental business of the country is on a sound and prosperous basis." Much as we may have liked Hoover, he spake with a forked tongue because that was the beginning of the Great Depression.

It's about the time of year to take stock of your garden fork and all the other lawn tools. Before you store them away for the winter, brush linseed oil over the entire tool surface—wood and metal. The metal will be protected against rust and the wood will be protected against moisture. Also the wooden handles will be much kinder and gentler to your hands next spring, thanks to the oil.

30

HAVE A BALL! Take your pick . . . ball bearings or ball point pens. On this day in 1794, the first commercial ball-bearing installation was made on the weather-vane atop the steeple of the Evangelical Lutheran Church of the Holy Trinity in Lancaster, Pennsylvania.

The ball point pen patent was obtained by John J. Loud for his invention. It was a writing pen with a rolling point. The year was 1888.

Have a ball with your pen even after it has dried up. Remove the pen barrel and there's a new use for the plastic barrel. Use a sharp knife to slice off spacers and plastic washers.

31

BOO! It's happy Halloween!

There is something magical about this day. Not just the witches, spooks, and goblins.

Here's a great halloween costume magically made from some otherwise throw-away stuff. Many things shipped to us are protected from damage by bubblepack material. Make your youngster a space suit from the bubble pack. Use clear tape to hold the sections together. Don't forget to provide easy-open flaps for emergencies. A motorcycle helmet caps off the perfect trick-or-treat costume . . . as if by magic!

NOVEMBER

- *You remembered the filters even before I mentioned 'em, didn't you?*

- *Inspect all the heating ducts to be sure you aren't losing expensive heat in the attic or basement.*

- *Be sure the snow blower is ready to go to work when Mother Nature covers you with a white blanket of snow.*

- *Protect your plants from the cold. Mulching is good.*

- *Be sure you have adequate attic ventilation. It's maybe more important in winter than in a hot summer.*

1

THE BARE FACTS! In 1953, the first issue of *Playboy* magazine was published by Hugh Hefner. The attraction wasn't the scantily clad models but, according to many husbands who bought the publication, "They really have great articles!"

Even if you aren't centerfold material, you may wish to become a stripper . . . of furniture, that is. But many people wonder when it's right to strip a piece of furniture. Here are some times not to strip:

First, try cleaning. Often furniture is coated with wax and in time the wax picks up and holds all sorts of dust, dirt, and grime. Usually mineral spirits paint thinner on a rag will remove the wax and thus the other gunk.

If the old finish is sound but has just lost its gloss, you can probably apply a new coat over the old.

If you're going to paint and the old paint or any other type finish is sound, don't strip.

2

This day in 1952 marked the first time in which the deep freezing technique was used in a heart operation.

If you use your freezer for more mundane things, like keeping the frozen fish sticks in that state, you should make sure the freezer compartment is at the proper temperature. Keep it between 0°F and 5°F. The refrigerator part is usually best kept at around 35°F.

3

DEWEY DEFEATS TRUMAN . . . ALMOST! On this date in 1948, the *Chicago Tribune* came out with a banner headline proclaiming Thomas E. Dewey the victor in the race for president. He was a heavy favorite. However, when all the votes were in, Harry S Truman had pulled the upset of the century.

If you have bumper stickers on your car following an election, there are better ways to remove them than with a Bowie knife.

One weird way is to smear mayonnaise over the sticker. The goo will soak through the sticker and you can peel it right off. Cold cream will do the same thing. (There's no truth to the thought that the cold cream will remove wrinkles in the bumper.) A spray lubricant will also work.

You do want to get these stickers off as soon as possible after the election so nobody will know you backed such an obvious loser. Besides, those old stickers can make your Edsel look bad.

4

WAGONS HO! After only six months of travel, the first emigrant wagon train made it to California on this day in 1841.

Although the little red wagon that Junior plays with is quite a bit different, it will do its share when you're laying floor tiles. Load the wagon with tiles and you can pull the tiles along as you work instead of having to make trips back for more.

5

The first stereo radio broadcast was made on this date in 1955. Radio does more than just bring the news and entertainment into the handy home. Anytime you'll be working on electricity, you'll certainly want to be sure there's no current to the circuit on which you're working.

If you don't have a helper to tell you when you trip the right circuit breaker or remove the proper fuse, plug a radio into an outlet on that circuit. With the volume turned up loud enough for you to hear, you'll know you got the right switch when the sound goes off.

6

The year was 1928. The first flasher sign was installed on four sides of the *New York Times* building. The moving messages were made possible by 14,800 bulbs.

Can you imagine how much trouble it would be to change a burned out bulb on a cold November day? If you have just a few exterior bulbs around your house, why not change them all at the beginning of winter. Otherwise, you know that one or more will burn out sometime during winter, probably on the coldest day.

You can still use the old bulbs in fixtures inside.

If you didn't do this and find there's a burned out bulb, go ahead and change all of them because another one is probably going to burn out next week.

7

RHYME TIME: The very first Burma-Shave signs were put up along two roads outside of Minneapolis in 1925. Eventually, these roadside rhymes were nationwide. Most had a series of six signs a couple of car lengths apart.

One that I still remember from when I was a kid was on the way to my Grandma's house:

> A MAN
> A MISS
> A CAR . . . A CURVE
> HE KISSED THE MISS
> AND MISSED THE CURVE
> BURMA-SHAVE

Shaving cream, no matter what the brand, has many uses for the home handyperson. Spray some on your hands before starting a messy project. Work the stuff into your hands and it becomes like an invisible glove. The grime and gunk will wash away much easier.

If you didn't do that ahead of time, aerosol shave cream makes a good waterless cleaner for your hands. Wipe it off with a rag or paper towel.

A roll of paper towels and a can of shaving cream are good additions to the trunk of your car for roadside repairs.

Shaving cream can also do a number on some carpet spots.

8

HELP FOR WHAT'S BUGGING YOU! On this day in 1910, W. M. Frost of Washington state received a patent on a device that was supposed to electrocute insects.

While the electronic bug zappers that you see on patios really do work at night, there's an electronic device that doesn't work: the ultrasonic device. These are supposed to emit a signal that is too high-pitched for us two-legged critters to hear, but that is said to drive insects crazy, or at least drive them away. However, recent research from Texas A&M University found that these sounds had no effect on pests. Ultrasound also has no effect on rodents.

9

LIGHTS OUT! In 1965, there was a massive power outage that blacked out the Northeastern United States and parts of Canada. It hit the New York City area right in the middle of rush hour.

When there's a blackout that covers your entire neighborhood, there's not much you can do about it but wait until the utility company can get things back on line.

One thing you should do, however, is to turn off as many things as you can so that when the power comes back on everything doesn't come on at once. Otherwise, all of that demand for power coming at one time could overload your home electrical system and blow fuses or trip circuit breakers.

After you've done that, you can just sit down and watch TV by candlelight.

10

Educational television took a big step in the right direction with the debut of "Sesame Street" on this date in 1969. One of its leading characters is Big Bird, a fine feathered friend indeed. If you'd like to do something nice for a family of feathered friends in your neighborhood, how about a nice house? An old rural mailbox can be mounted on a high pole, and with the door open, it won't be any time before a bird family starts a nest inside.

11

It's now called Veterans Day. The day used to be called Armistice Day—declaring an end to World War I. Signing the declaration was done with a flair in 1918. It happened on the eleventh day of the eleventh month at the eleventh hour, eleventh minute.

One of the hazards of signing official documents is that of getting ink stains where they shouldn't be. Often a ballpoint pen stain on fabric or carpet will respond to hair spray. It's worth a try. If that doesn't get the job done, try a fabric spot remover solution. With any solvent, test it out first on an obscure spot.

12

The first hotel for dogs, Kennelworth, opened in New York City on this day in 1975. The 116 rooms offer different color schemes and are air-conditioned. You don't have to have a major credit card but you must have proof of rabies and distemper shots. (They do accept credit cards, however.)

If Fido keeps knocking over his water dish, here's a tip: take an old saucepan with a metal handle. Straighten the handle out so that it sticks straight up. Then use the hang-up hole in the handle to fit over a fastener driven into the wall. That way, the pan rests on the floor, but is secured.

13

It was 1964, and the medical news of the day was that Cassius Clay (or was he Muhammad Ali by then?) had a hernia operation. Probably from lifting his wallet.

There are many lifting chores around the home and not doing these properly can result in hernias or other injuries. First, when picking up the load, never bend at the waist. Lower yourself at the knees. Keep your back straight and let your legs do the work of raising you and the object. Hold the item being lifted as close to your body as possible. And my favorite: get somebody else to do the lifting!

14

BLOOD TRANSFUSION DAY! No, you don't have to go get one. This day marks the day in 1666 when the first blood transfusion was performed. It was not, however, performed on humans. A Dr. Croone used a pair of dogs for his experiment.

Wherever the blood comes from, blood spots on a carpet are hard to get out. As with most stains, the sooner you get after blood the better. First dampen the spot with cool water. Sponge with a clean cloth or paper towel. If you get a yellowish stain where the blood was, apply a few drops of hydrogen peroxide. Blot this up after only a minute with a towel dipped in cool water.

Another method is to first sprinkle the area with meat tenderizer and then blot with cool water.

A 50/50 mix of white vinegar and water will usually help get rid of such stains.

Remember, always try any stain remover on some obscure spot first to be sure it does no harm to the carpet.

15

WHO? Today is George Spelvin Day. On November 15, 1886, George Spelvin was created. He appeared in a Broadway play and has since appeared in thousands of Broadway performances. The name was created to appear in the playbill to hide the fact that an actor was performing in more than one part. Female actors used Georgetta. There are other such fictitious names employed in the theatre for this purpose but this one is probably the most used.

Just as in the theatre, everything may not be as it seems in the home improvement field. So before you sign on the dotted line to allow some company to make some improvement around the place, find out about the company or contractor. Maybe you think that if the work doesn't come out the way you expected, you'll just refuse to pay. Many times with some types of contracts you still have to pay or you could lose your home. The law may be on the side of the shoddy or even crooked tradesman.

There are also times when a tradesman will discount your note to a legitimate lending institution so that even if the contractor or company has disappeared, you still legally owe the note.

Sometimes if you've signed the wrong kind of document with the wrong kind of folks, you'll even have to pick up the tab for unpaid materials. That means you'll have paid twice for part of the job.

Guarantees are only as good as the company and may not apply to the materials manufacturer or the lending institution. You could be totally unhappy with a lousy job, but nonpayment on your part could cost you your home.

Be sure before you sign away your home.

16

While fingernail painting goes back for centuries, it's only in the past fifty years or so that exotic colors came into vogue. On November 24, 1907, however, a beautician named Mavis Rhea Gilford of Chicago introduced glow-in-the-dark polish. It wasn't a big hit, although now it would probably be quite popular. Mavis Rhea was born about seventy-five years too soon.

Fingernail polish has more uses than just for fingernails.

If a screw or bolt keeps coming loose from vibration, smear some polish on the threads and install the fastener. When the polish sets up, the vibration won't cause a problem.

Coat the bottom of the rim on a can of shaving cream to keep it from rusting and leaving a ring on the vanity top.

A BB gun hole in a window pane can be filled with clear polish. Just put a dab on and let dry and then repeat until the hole is filled. Because of the many colors available, polish can also be used to repair such a hole in stained glass . . . maybe even if the glass is in glow-in-the-dark colors.

After the polish is gone, refill the tiny bottle with leftover paint from your project and you have the color and brush for quick touch-ups.

17

The first dental hygienist course was offered on this day in the year 1913 at the Fones Clinic in Bridgeport, Connecticut. Thirty-three women enrolled and twenty-seven of those graduated. If you know a dental hygienist, ask for the tools of the trade when they are no longer fit for use in the chair. The scraper, picks, and mirrors will find many handy uses around the home and shop. For example, the mirror can help you see in tough places where you're working.

18

On this day in 1963, Ma Bell introduced the "Touch-Tone" phone. They claimed that the time for dialing a number was ten seconds and with the buttons it took only five seconds. So if you make 100 calls per month, you'd save 8 minutes and 20 seconds . . . getting to those busy signals much quicker.

While the phone companies are proud of their *Yellow Pages*, you can make your own directory. As you run across suppliers, tradesmen, repair people, and contractors, start compiling a listing of the good ones. Not only will it help you, it's information you can share with your friends and relatives. *(See beginning of this book.)*

19

The most famous speech made by President Abe Lincoln, the Gettysburg Address, was made on this day in 1863. It was said that he wrote his speech on the back of an envelope on the way to Gettysburg.

Another handy use for an envelope is as a dispenser for insecticide powder. Put the powder into the envelope and seal it. (BUT, DO NOT LICK THE FLAP. USE A DAMP PAPER TOWEL.) Snip off a corner of the envelope. Crimp the edges so the envelope takes in air. Now you can slip the snipped corner under the baseboard and poof the dust in to where the bugs are. It will also get powder into other tough-to-reach spots.

20

THE CRIMINAL LOOK On this day in 1914, it became a requirement that all passports contain a photograph of the person to whom it was issued. . .even though no passport picture has ever resembled the person.

Hopefully, your photographic efforts turn out better than passport photos. One good use for those 35mm film cans is as a camp-out firelighter kit. Put a few matches plus a couple of birthday candle stubs in the can. It is waterproof when closed. This kit is easily carried in your pocket and when needed, will get the fire going in a hurry.

21

LIGHT PLEASE! Just in time to save the planet, M. F. Gale invented the cigar lighter and was awarded a patent for same on this day in 1871.

Cigar smokers are not very popular in some quarters because of the odor and the smoke. However, if you have a white water ring on your coffee table, cigar ashes can do a great job of curing this problem. Cover the spot with the ashes and then pour on some cooking oil. Use a cotton cloth and rub and the water mark will gradually fade away. When it's gone, wipe the surface clean and then apply your regular furniture polish. Cigarette ashes will also work but not as well as cigar ashes.

22

HELP! Back in 1906, the distress signal SOS was adopted on this day. It does not stand for "Save Our Ship" as some believe. In the

Morse code, it's just an easy signal to send by wireless . . . dot-dot-dot, dash-dash-dash, dot-dot-dot.

When you need to send out a distress signal in connection with the project you have under way, there is a simple way. The code to remember is 800. Many companies have 800 numbers you can call free to ask for help. Major appliance manufacturers, building materials makers, and lots of other companies and groups have 1-800-help lines. We have supplied a partial list of helpful 800 numbers on page 3.

23

PUT ANOTHER NICKEL IN! On this day in 1889, the very first jukebox was installed. It was placed in the Palais Royale Saloon in San Francisco. A nickel isn't worth much anymore and all our money is worth less because of inflation. However, a dime is still a pretty good emergency pocket screwdriver. But don't use enough force to damage the dime. That's against the law. And besides, the damaged dime may not work in the pay phone or vending machine.

24

IT'S YOUR MOVE! On this day in 1926, a chess game was started by mail between Dr. Munro MacLennan and Lawrence Grant. Since they only made a single move each time they corresponded, the game went on for over fifty years. It was never finished but was called off when one of the contestants died. The fax machine certainly could have speeded things up.

If you'd like to make your own nuts and bolts chess set, here are the plans I used for mine. Be my guest.

After you look over the easy-to-make pieces, you may find that you have many of the nuts and bolts in your garage or workshop. If you don't, your hardware dealer will have everything. In fact, you may find other interesting items that will allow you to change my designs.

All these pieces come in various sizes. You can make a fairly large set or a very small one.

Here's how I put mine together.

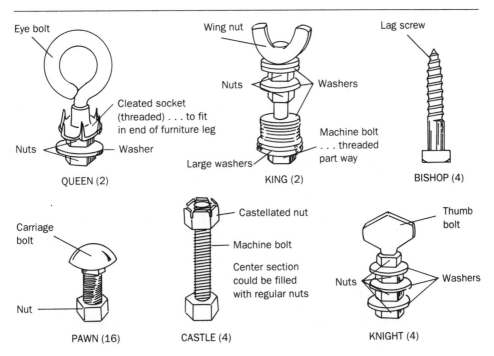

After you have decided on your design, use an adhesive that will glue metal to make the parts stick together. Spread the cement on threads and on other parts that go together.

Spray half the pieces with black metal paint and you're all set to play.

P.S. You'll need a board. You could buy one at the variety story or you could be creative and make one from leftover scraps of vinyl flooring. Just pick two contrasting colors and glue squares to a piece of plywood.

25 **THE SHARP TONGUE!** On November 25, 1817, the first sword swallowing exhibition took place. It was a cut-throat competition to see who was best. If you'll be sharpening your sword using a file, there is a chance you could slice a finger. Add a plastic coffee can lid between the handle and the file to act as a hand guard.

26 **CLANG, CLANG, CLANG WENT THE TROLLEY!** Public street car service in New York City started on this day in 1832. Many cities at one time had the street car as their means of public transportation.

Then the bus came along and the tracks were paved over. It might have been better if we had preserved the trolley systems for use today.

Certainly we all wish our great grandparents had preserved all that old furniture they had. Antique as well as good old furniture can bring big bucks. Furniture from the '20s, '30s, '40s, and even the '50s and '60s is very popular now and promises to be even more valuable in the future.

Most people know to take care of antiques. But people with this newer-than-antique furniture may not exercise the care that Chippendale owners do. And they may not reap the benefits later on. Here are some things to do to take care of your old furniture.

- Loose joints may lead to bigger damage. Stress will loosen other joints and pretty soon either the entire piece falls apart or parts break.

- Protect your furniture from long daily exposure to direct sunlight. Sun will break down the finish and can lighten the color of wood.

- Protect the finish from a too-dry house in the winter. See that furniture doesn't sit in the path of hot air from the vents.

- Armor-coat the surfaces with either a good furniture polish or with wax. Avoid waxy buildup though, because it can collect dirt, which can act as an abrasive, and moisture, which can leave water spots.

- Be sure the items that sit on the furniture are padded to prevent surface damage.

- Periodically inspect edges for splits and veneer for loosening. These are things that may get worse if not stopped at an early stage.

Enjoy your old furniture but also treat it right, and maybe when *you* become an antique, it'll take care of you when it sells for megabucks!

27

GRAND OPENING! Back in 1910, the then largest railway terminal in the world had its grand opening. It was Penn Station in New York City.

If the grand opening to your backyard is a sliding glass patio door, here's something to think about. Eventually, if you have such a sliding glass door, it will become a nonsliding door!

Your problem may be as simple as grit or a small rock in the lower track. Take a look. Also check both upper and lower tracks for burrs or bends. Use an abrasive to remove burrs. Try a mallet and wood block to cure bends.

If a bent track can't be straightened, you might be able to replace the entire track—if you can track down a track.

Most such doors roll on bottom rollers. Usually, if you'll look at the edges of the slider, you'll see two screws. The lower screw should adjust the roller up and down. A few turns of the screws on each edge to raise the door may solve the problem.

If not, these adjusting screws will retract the rollers to allow you to lift the door completely out to examine the rollers. Be careful, as such doors are heavy. Examine the rollers. Sometimes they just need lubrication. If they need to be replaced, your hardware store or home center is likely to have what you need.

Replacement doors of wood or fiberglass are popular. They have a fixed side, but the door side swings instead of sliding. They're more energy efficient and more secure than the sliding type.

28

In 1925, the Grand Ole Opry debuted on radio station WSM in Nashville. The Opry, the station, and Nashville are all still going strong. Minnie Pearl, an Opry mainstay, always wore her hat with the price tag hanging down. Sometimes price tags are hard to get rid of, particularly the stick-on kind. If light oil won't harm the article, use a spray lubricant. It works almost every time.

29

NOW YOU SEE IT, NOW YOU DON'T. On this date in 1775, the Committee for Secret Correspondence was formed. Their purpose was to correspond with friends of the United States in other countries using invisible ink, which was introduced by Silas Deane. He also introduced the Dick Tracy Secret Decoder Ring.

Invisibility is also helpful to the do-it-yourselfer because one of the secrets of being a good handyperson is being able to hide your mistakes.

OLD HOUSE TIP

Most moldings in old houses are made from plaster. It has a character not found in wood molding. If you want to add molding, however, wood can be made to look like plaster . . . just coat it with gesso. This is a product found in art supply stores.

Paint can hide bad patching jobs or cheap wood and can even cover up the streaks and lap marks of a sloppy coat of paint. Molding hides badly sawed tops and bottoms of paneling that you put up to hide a crummy-looking wall.

Molding also hides the gaps between kitchen cabinets and the floor, ceiling, or walls. Fabric or wallpaper can hide a badly textured or cracked wall. And pictures and wall mirrors hide all sorts of wall worries.

Indoor-outdoor carpet can hide all the cracks in the badly finished concrete porch or patio.

A suspended ceiling system will hide the cracks or even the hole you made when you stepped through the ceiling when you were in the attic. These ceilings also hide plumbing pipes and electrical wires on a basement ceiling.

Now you know some Super Handyman secrets . . . and it feels good to get that confession off my chest. And, speaking of my chest, anybody got any good ideas on how to hide a tatoo on my chest that has an old girlfriend's name on it?

30

CHICKEN LITTLE WAS RIGHT! On November 30, 1954, a meteorite struck a human being for the first time. The strikee was Elizabeth Hodges of Alabama. The 8½-pound chunk of stone came right through the roof of her home. Speaking of the roof, any time you have a new roof installed using composition shingles, stick a few leftovers in the trunk of your car. Sometime when you're spinning the wheels of your car on an icy or muddy patch, slip the shingles under the wheels for added traction to get you going.

DECEMBER

- *It's again time to be sure your smoke alarms are still ready to protect you.*

- *Keep your car battery fully charged. Cold starts are harder so you need all the juice the battery can give.*

- *Inspect the snow tires to be sure they'll be ready.*

- *After a snowstorm, gently remove snow that is weighing down the boughs, using a broom or your hands.*

- *Get the Christmas lights out for a safety inspection.*

- *Trim evergreens and use the cuttings to form Christmas wreathes and garlands.*

- *Hold a candle up close to wall outlets to check for cold air leaks.*

- *. . . and about those filters?*

1

THIS DATE IN HISTORY

In 1956, the U.S. Army decided to move into the twentieth century. On this day they announced plans to do away with the last mule unit.

Unless you're stubborn as a mule, you won't mind learning a new trick. Before lighting the next fire in the fireplace, remove the grate and line the fireplace floor with aluminum foil. The shiny surface will reflect more heat out into the room while making the fire seem brighter. Then the big reward is the next day: instead of having to scoop up the ashes, you just roll up the foil and the cleanup is done.

2

THE CHAIN GANG!

On this day in 1942, the first nuclear chain reaction was created. Chains are often helpful in securing our property. You can fix two sections of chain together even without a connector link. Just use a padlock to join the two to form a longer chain. Another way to accomplish this same feat is to use a large nut and bolt through the end link of both sections. It may not be as strong as a connector link, but if that's all you have, it'll help.

3

HAVE A HEART

In 1967, Dr. Christian Neethling Barnard performed the first successful human heart transplant.

The Christmas tree transplant has become more popular with many ecology-minded people. The idea is to have a living tree that can be moved outdoors after the holidays and transplanted into the landscape.

This is a great idea but you have to be sure that the species of tree is one that will grow in your area. Your nurseryman can help on that score.

It's a good idea to dig the hole for the transplant before freezing weather hits. Digging in frozen ground is difficult. Cover the hole with a sheet of plywood so nobody falls in and breaks a leg.

After Christmas, when it's time to take the tree down, don't just move it from the warmth of the house to the cold outside all at once. It should be done gradually so there's not so great a shock. If you have an unused room in the house that isn't heated, that should be the first stop for the tree. After a day, move it to the garage for another day or two. Then on the next warmish day, move it out to the hole and plant it.

If you didn't dig the hole, wait until the ground thaws. To keep the tree alive while waiting to plant it, mound dirt and mulch around the root ball.

4

GET OFF MY BACK! Every year about this time the environmentalists are on my case because I tell how to preserve a cut Christmas tree. They say that cutting so many trees is raping the land of a natural resource. They say the forests must be preserved.

The Christmas tree industry has nothing to do with the forests. Christmas trees are a crop just like wheat or cotton. They are planted, grown, harvested, and then replanted again. They're not grown in the forests. Of course, there are individuals that sneak out into the forest and chop down a tree and the environmentalists have a gripe against them.

If you wish to buy an artificial tree because it's a good investment or because you don't like the mess of a cut tree, fine. Or, if you like the idea of a living tree that can be planted in the yard after the holidays, great! But don't feel guilty about buying a cut tree, because you're no more depleting the natural resources of the world than if you ate breakfast food this morning.

In fact, if Euell Gibbons were still alive, he might even eat a few Christmas trees.

5

I'LL DRINK TO THAT! On this day in 1933, Prohibition was repealed. Since people no longer needed to make their own "white lightning," as the amateur distillers of illegal booze called their product, they needed to find uses for those big old oak barrels. Somebody came up with the idea of sawing them in half to become planters. If you do this, it's a good idea to char the inside surfaces with the flame from a propane torch before planting.

6

I THINK THAT I SHALL NEVER SEE . . . This is the birthday of Joyce Kilmer, whose most famous poem is "Trees." At this time of year, the only tree most of us are interested in is the Christmas tree. Picking out the right tree is important and here are the facts.

Have you bought your Christmas tree yet? If you haven't, I've got some tips on picking out the freshest possible tree. After all, the trees on the lot were probably cut a month ago and could be getting dried out. A too-dry tree can be a fire hazard. So, before you buy, give it the "scratch-whack-flex" test.

For the "scratch" test, reach in to the trunk and use your thumb nail to scratch the bark. A fresh tree will reveal a juicy green underside to the bark.

The "whack" test requires that you pick up the tree by the main trunk. Raise it up about ten inches and bring it sharply back down against the ground. If the "whack!" causes a shower of needles from the tree, that means the tree is pretty dry, so move on to another.

The flex test involves your bending a few of the branches. If they're brittle, the tree is dry. Of course, be careful not to break any very big branches or the lot attendant may break one of your limbs.

After you find a fresh tree and get it home, saw off the bottom half inch or so from the trunk and put the tree into a bucket of water until time to take it into the house.

7

THIS DAY IN HISTORY

The Japanese bombing of Pearl Harbor occurred in 1941. This led to the United States entry into World War II.

CHRISTMAS TREE FIREPROOFING

Here's a spray-on fireproofing formula that needs to be applied just before the tree is brought into the house. Start with 1/2 gallon of water and add 1/2 cup of ammonium sulfate, 1/4 cup boric acid powder, and 1 tablespoon of borax. Spray this liberally on the tree and when dry, apply a second coat.

8

When it's time to bring the Christmas tree inside, start it off right with this magic formula. Start with a gallon of hot water. Add 4 tablespoons of horticultural iron powder available where you buy gardening supplies. Pour in 2 cups of crystal clear corn syrup. Next, add 4 teaspoons of liquid laundry bleach. Stir to mix.

This stuff goes into the tree stand. The tree will drink it and not dry out so rapidly and thus, not become a fire hazard.

Before putting the tree into the stand, cut off any caked-over area on the bottom of the trunk.

To help the tree to be able to drink more readily, drill a hole up through the center of the trunk and stuff this with cotton. This will act as a wick and bring in more water.

When the magic formula is gone, keep the liquid level in the tree stand up by adding warm water on a daily basis.

The average seven-foot tree will drink almost two quarts of liquid per day.

9

HERE'S LOOKING AT YOU, SANTA! Here's something fun you and the family can make . . .

INFINITY MIRROR

The "infinity mirror" has lights that seem to go very deep into the frame. It's particularly dramatic in a darkened room. However, when the mirror lights are off and the room lights are on, it's just like an ordinary mirror. The basic idea is that there is a one way mirror at the front of the unit. Behind this and spaced all around the frame are tiny lights. Behind that is another mirror. The lights reflect against the mirrors which in turn reflect against each other which gives you the effect of depth.

Our model was made with leftovers: scrap lumber, a string of Christmas tree lights, two panes of glass, and some leftover reflective film designed to control sun and reflect it back out of your house. When the highly reflective film is applied to glass, that glass becomes a one way mirror.

Here are the components and their sequence, starting at the back.

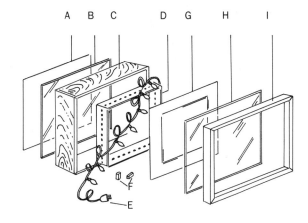

A. Cardboard backing piece painted black.

B. Glass to which sun control film has been applied. This film comes in several densities. Get the most reflective density available (80% or greater). The black backing makes this into the equivalent of a regular mirror.

C. Outer frame made from 1"x4" boards. This frame should be big enough to leave 1" space all around inner frame D. This space houses the electric cord. This outer frame can be stained or painted to suite your decor.

D. Inner frame made from ½" or thinner slats with holes drilled every inch on all 4 sides. Drill holes to accommodate sockets in string of lights and let the number of lights control the size of this frame. Start your basic construction with this unit.

E. Christmas tree lights: use a string of 100 or 1 pair of 50-light strings. We used assorted colors because that's what was available, but you'll attain a more dramatic effect with all white lights.

F. Blocks of wood glued at all corners to hold inner and outer frames in position.

G. Posterboard mat cut to hide gap between inner and outer frames.

H. Outer glass also has sun control film applied to it.

I. Frame of molding holds glass in place and gives finished look to front.

All of the components within the frame that are visible should be black. Be sure to leave a hole in the back for the wire and plug.

There is the basic idea, but you can adapt it to your own design. Use more lights or make the frame oblong instead of square. You can use the basic idea as a wall hanging or lay it flat and make an infinity table. In fact, go into a mod furniture store and look at some of the store bought models for ideas. Also, look at the price tag (from $200), and go home to reflect on how you'll save by doing it yourself.

10

FAKING IT?

If you elect to have an artificial tree, assembly will be easier if you coat the tip ends of the branches with petroleum jelly before poking them in place. This also makes disassembly go faster.

11

Maybe you've discovered the Christmas candy already. Maybe you're getting a ten-speed for Christmas. And maybe it's time for some exercise. . . .

SUPERCYCLE EXERBIKE

Here's what you can do with the old bicycle in the garage that's just collecting dust. If it's a 1-speed or if the gears are inside the rear hub, you could convert it to an exerbike, probably using scraps and hardware you have on hand. Here's how I did it . . . but keep in mind, you can adapt or change or improve to suit yourself. I just used things I had on hand and came up with this . . .

> MATERIALS
> 3/4 inch plywood
> 2 mounting plates (8 inch)
> 4 L-shaped shelf braces
> 2 screen door springs
> 2 eye bolts
> 2 S-hooks
> 1 metal rod (1/8 inch diameter)
> 20 stove bolts* and nuts
> 2 extra bike axle nuts
> 1 wooden spool

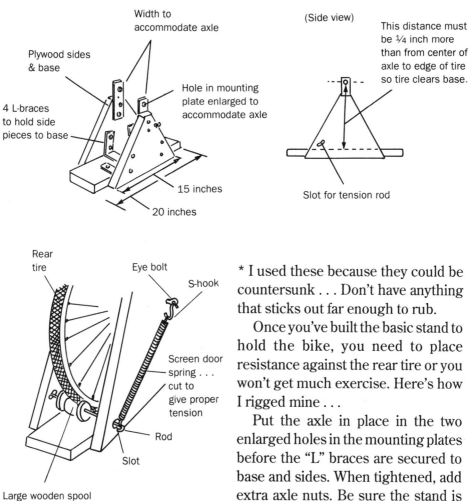

Width to accommodate axle

Plywood sides & base

4 L-braces to hold side pieces to base

Hole in mounting plate enlarged to accommodate axle

15 inches

20 inches

(Side view)

This distance must be ¼ inch more than from center of axle to edge of tire so tire clears base.

Slot for tension rod

Rear tire

Eye bolt

S-hook

Screen door spring . . . cut to give proper tension

Rod

Slot

Large wooden spool

* I used these because they could be countersunk . . . Don't have anything that sticks out far enough to rub.

Once you've built the basic stand to hold the bike, you need to place resistance against the rear tire or you won't get much exercise. Here's how I rigged mine . . .

Put the axle in place in the two enlarged holes in the mounting plates before the "L" braces are secured to base and sides. When tightened, add extra axle nuts. Be sure the stand is tight, solid, and secure . . . or you may be riding off thru the wall.

Happy pedalling!

12   THIS DATE IN HISTORY

Today is Poinsettia Day. Dr. Joel Roberts Poinsett introduced the Central American plant to the U.S. The poinsettia has become the Christmas flower in the U.S. Pretty as they may be, many Christmas plants are not good to have in a home with pets. The mistletoe and holly used in some decorations are toxic to pets. So is the Christmas rose.

13

> ### OLD HOUSE TIP
>
> Many colonial homes fea-
> tured stenciling. You don't
> need to buy stenciling
> paper. Use part of a brown
> paper bag sprayed with a
> coat of shellac.

14

THE GIFT WRAPPED TREE

With the tree not even up, why would we talk about taking it down? As you know, when it's time to haul the tree outside, you will always leave a trail of needles throughout the house. You can also get stabbed by the dried needles. There is a way to prevent this *if* the tree isn't up yet.

Get a big throwaway plastic painter's drop cloth and cut a hole in the center of the plastic. Poke the tree trunk through the hole before installing it into the stand. Fold the plastic on all four sides and cover it with the decorative tree skirt, but leave enough room to add water to the stand.

After Christmas, unfold the plastic and bring all four corners up to the top of the tree. You now have the tree in the bag and can carry it out without losing any needles or getting stabbed. It's quicker, too.

You just have to be smarter than the tree.

15

BREAK A LEG! About this time of year, folks do a lot of ladder climbing. They're either putting up Christmas decorations or pruning trees. About this time the following week, these same folks appear with casts on their legs. Ladder climbing must be done carefully.

First, inspect the ladder each time before going up. Be certain a straight ladder is on solid ground and that it's level. Have it angled at a rate of one foot out for every four feet up to where it rests.

Never go higher than the second step from the top. Use both hands when climbing, hoisting the tools up after you're there. When working, use one hand to hold with at all times. Always keep your body between the side rails.

When sawing a limb, be sure it can't fall on you. Wear goggles if sawdust will be falling on your face. And don't use the limb you're cutting to hold onto or both you and the limb will come crashing down.

If you're going to break a leg, it's much more chic to do it while skiing.

16

FREE GREENERY

If you have evergreens that need to be pruned, save the trimmings to use as Christmas greenery on the mantle and other places.

17

Not that I'm nagging, but here's another health do-it-yourself project for you, your dad, and Arnold Schwarzenegger—or Cher.

WEIGHT BENCH

If you have a barbell set, you've probably always wanted a weight bench. This one is designed to safely hold only 100 pounds in weights. However, you must insure that the bench is sturdy and safe by hand picking good materials and by using your skills in building it.

★ *Also be sure to consult your doctor before starting any exercise program.*

BUILDING THE BENCH: All the pieces marked "A" are 2x4's. The rest of the frame is of 2x6 material. The bench top is made of 2 pieces of 3/4 inch plywood 48 inches long and 10¾ inches wide. Secure one top piece to the side 2x6's using 8d nails and a good wood glue. Use nails about every 6 to 8 inches.

Attach second top piece of plywood with glue and #8 1¼ inch flat head screws from underneath, using 2 pair at each end.

Now cut 2x6 end blocks to fit between the 2x6 side pieces. Glue and use 10d nails. There is a small ¾ inch plywood piece at each end and on the bottom of the bench attached with 8d nails and glue, but don't install it until the legs are in place.

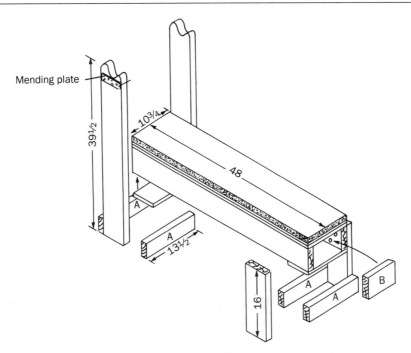

The weight supports need to be cut in the configuration shown. Use the diameter of the bar of your barbell set as a guide. The rounded slot for the barbell should be about 2½ inches in from the edge. The 5-inch mending plate is very important.

Attach weight supports and legs with ⅜"x4" carriage bolts with nuts and washers. Use 3 for each piece, making sure your pilot holes miss the end block. Be sure to make bottoms of supports and legs all the same distance from bottom of bench so the unit is level. Use a square too.

The 2x4 pieces are attached to the legs and supports using 10d nails.

The foam pad should be at least an inch thick.

To finish the unit, sand all edges and coat the wood with a clear sealer. Cover the foam with fabric.

See you at Muscle Beach!

18

Rather than drive a new nail in every year for each Christmas stocking, do your mantle a favor and install a tiny cup hook for each stocking. The hooks can be painted to match the mantle and left in place year round without being noticeable.

19

THIS DATE IN HISTORY

In 1732, Ben Franklin published the first edition of *Poor Richard's Almanack,* the mother of all almanacs . . . if you don't like this almanac, blame it on Ben.

Certainly we can blame Ben for his part in discovering electricity and creating the frustrations many are having on this day because of a string of Christmas tree lights that won't work.

When you packed them away last year, all the Christmas lights were working. Now when you take them out, none will come on.

This is just one of the Twelve Laws of Christmas.

Let's look for the problem, and as we do, we'll also check to make sure the string of lights is going to be safe. A faulty set of lights could cause a fire.

First, inspect the plug. Then go over every inch of the wiring to see if there's any insulation worn away or if there are cuts in the wire. If you have to tape over a bare spot, you can get green electrical tape which won't even show. Check all the wires where they enter the sockets. They tend to pull loose here. If such wires can't be reinstalled, and many can't, you can snip out that entire socket and splice the wires together, making sure the connection is done properly and that it's taped over. Don't cut out more than a socket or two.

Use only lights specified for exterior use outside the house.

Be certain all the strings of lights are safe so that your house and tree are lit up from the lights and not from a house fire.

20

A QUICK SNOW JOB

If you're sure you won't get a white Christmas, here's a way to make your own snow for decorating the tree. Mix 2 cups of soap flakes and 2/3 cup of liquid starch with 4 tablespoons of water. Use a handheld rotary beater to whip the mix into a thick, frothy consistency. Add a few drops of blue food coloring as you beat to attain a snow-white look. Brush this on the tree and then sprinkle white glitter to give it an icy look.

21

Convert regular candles into something special for the holidays. Roll each candle individually between your hands. The heat will soften the wax on the outside. While they're warm, roll the candles in silver or gold glitter. The result is festive.

22

Spray paint pine cones to hang on the Christmas tree as decorations or to use in the centerpiece of a table.

23

I'M DREAMING OF A WHITE CHRISTMAS! If you woke up to a blanket of snow at your house, you should know that shoveling snow isn't as easy as it looks. Some studies show that shoveling the white stuff at a normal rate is as strenuous as running at 9 miles per hour. That's a fairly good marathon-runner's speed.

Make snow shoveling a bit easier with the right snow shovel. If you'll be buying a new one, get one with a long enough handle to provide good leverage. A too-short handle makes you have to work harder and this increases the risk of overexertion. Also look at the blade lift, the distance between the blade tip and the ground when the tool is lying flat. The higher the lift, the less effort for you.

Even with the right shovel, it's still work. Maybe the best idea is to get a snow blower or pay the neighbor's kid to do the job. Neither the blower nor the kid ever seem to have back problems or heart attacks.

24

When applying artificial snow to decorate windows, first spray a light coat of the non-stick aerosol cooking oil. When it's time to undecorate, the snow will wipe off like magic.

25

MERRY CHRISTMAS!

The only handy work today is to hope you're handy with the checkbook to pay for all the goodies.

26

OUT DAMN SPOT!

Christmas can take its toll on carpets. There are about as many things to spill as there are fleas on a junkyard dog. Different spills require different types of cleaners and different techniques. If, however, I had to give one word of advice for emergency treatment of a spill, that one word would be *blot*, B-L-O-T, blot.

Immediately blot any spill with an absorbent cloth or paper towel. Keep blotting and changing the cloth or towel. And then when you're tired of blotting, blot some more.

Once you've blotted up all the spill, you can use a proper cleaner or spot remover. Remember not to oversoak the carpet as you apply the cleaner. What do we do to prevent this? That's right, we continue to blot, blot, blot.

After the cleaning and blotting, place a thick pad of paper towel over the spot and press firmly down to blot and absorb any remaining liquid.

Blotting is a good first step for any kind of carpet. Blot the spot and it may never become a stain!

27

FOR THE BIRDS

A great use for the Christmas tree is to remove the decorations and redecorate with berries, popcorn, bread, and other things that birds can eat. Move the tree to the back yard and both you and the birds can enjoy it a little longer.

28

R. O. D. Sullivan became the first person to fly across the Atlantic Ocean 100 times on this date in 1942. Don't you wonder why?

Heat the blade of your snow shovel and rub a candle stub over the warm surface. The coat of wax left on the shovel makes the snow less likely to stick and you can fly through this chore.

29

This time of year, the fireplace is usually well used. Now, you don't have to be told not to stick your hand into the fire or you'll get burned. It doesn't take a rocket scientist to figure that out. But there are other ways for a fireplace to hurt you.

First of all, check inside the fireplace for cracks in the mortar joints. A gap could act as a sort of chimney and suck in a flame that could reach something combustible.

Inspect the flue or chimney looking for creosote buildup which can be a fire hazard.

A proper screen is a must to prevent embers from popping out on the carpet or wooden floors, bringing you more warmth than you want.

What you burn can be unsafe. Scrap lumber from an old building could have been painted with a lead-based paint. Smoke with lead particles is very unhealthy. Pressure-treated lumber throws off toxic fumes when burned. Even colored ink from newspaper and magazines is said to render cancer-causing smoke.

Finally, when cleaning out the ashes, be sure there aren't any glowing embers hidden in the ashes to start a fire in the garbage bin.

30

It's time to start thinking about those New Year's resolutions. One that you should make and keep is to check the batteries on your smoke alarm twice a year. In fact, New Year's Day and the Fourth of July would be good days to do this. Another popular way to remember this vital check is to do it on the two times per year that we change our clocks for daylight savings time. However you can best remember, make sure you do it. It could be a matter of life or death.

31

NEW YEAR'S EVE! One way that many people celebrate is to remove the old Christmas tree. If you didn't heed our suggestion made earlier this month about gift-wrapping the tree, here's another way to get the tree out of the house without the trail of needles.

Get a good supply of paper grocery bags and your pruning shears. Snip off a branch at a time, poking each into a bag as you go. When all that's left is the trunk, you have all the branches bagged for easy removal and the trunk is no problem.

What do you do with all this stuff? The branches and bags can go into your compost heap. If you have a chipping machine, convert the trunk into wood chips. Resist the temptation to burn any of this in the fireplace. It burns too fast to make much heat and because it flares up, it can be dangerous. Most trees used for Christmas also throw off a lot of creosote which isn't all that desirable.

INDEX

INDEX

INDEX